Grow Over It!

Overcoming the Obstacles in Your Life
Through a Godly Perspective

Amanda Conner

Copyright © 2021 by **Amanda Conner**

All rights reserved. No part of this publication may be reproduced, distributed, or transmitted in any form or by any means, without prior written permission.

Scripture quotations marked (AMP) are taken from the Amplified® Bible (AMP), copyright © 2015 by The Lockman Foundation. Used by permission. www.Lockman.org.

Scripture quotations marked (BSB) are taken from The Holy Bible, Berean Study Bible, BSB. Copyright ©2016 by Bible Hub. Used by Permission. All Rights Reserved Worldwide.

Scripture quotations marked (CSB) are taken from The Christian Standard Bible. Copyright © 2017 by Holman Bible Publishers. Used by permission

Scripture quotations marked (EHV) are taken from the Holy Bible, Evangelical Heritage Version® (EHV®) © 2019 Wartburg Project, Inc. All rights reserved. Used by permission.

Scripture quotations marked (EXB) are taken from The Expanded Bible. Copyright © 2011 by Thomas Nelson. Used by permission. All rights reserved.

Scripture quotations marked (KJV) are taken from the King James Bible. Accessed on Bible Gateway. www.BibleGateway.com.

Scripture quotations marked (NASB) are taken from the New American Standard Bible ® (NASB), copyright © 1960, 1962, 1963, 1968, 1971, 1972, 1973, 1975, 1977, 1995 by The Lockman Foundation. Used by permission. www.Lockman.org.

Scripture quotations marked (NIV) are taken from the Holy Bible, New International Version. Copyright © 1973, 1978, 1984, 2011 by Biblica, Inc.® Used by permission. All rights reserved worldwide.

Scripture quotations marked (NKJV) are taken from the New King James Version®. Copyright © 1982 by Thomas Nelson, Inc. Used by permission. All rights reserved.

Scripture quotations marked (NLT) are taken from the Holy Bible, New Living Translation, copyright © 1996, 2004, 2015 by Tyndale House Foundation. Used by permission of Tyndale House Publishers, Inc., Carol Stream, Illinois 60188. All rights reserved.

Grow Over It! / Amanda Conner

Dear Dad,

I finished it. I took your advice and didn't become stingy with what God gave me. Your words, "Hey Baby, you can do it!" still awaken courage as they sit clearly on the mantle of my heart. You made your ceiling my floor. May I honor God and be worthy of the call we both answered. From one generation to the next—I'll keep going!

Amanda

To Constance, my dearest friend,

Thank you for being you and for supporting me throughout this process, truly being a Barnabas to my soul. Your encouragement and talent have been wind to the sails of my dreams. Thank you. All my love,

Amanda

CONTENTS

Over the Wall 3
Dreaming God-Given Dreams 19
Are You Abiding? 35
Taking Off Emotional Armor 51
A Lifestyle of Prayer 73
The Armor of God 89
Hostile Environments 105
Shadowboxing 127
Growing Over It in Hope 147
Choose Trust 161
Notes 163
About the Author 167

INTRODUCTION

Over the Wall

I will never forget the day someone walked up to me and said, "Wow, you sure can preach for a girl!" It was the beginning of a beautiful relationship between the challenge of being who God called me to be and the reality of what it means to face countless contrary perspectives—and rise above them.

Challenges. Obstacles. Disappointments. These obstacles are always present in our walk with God. In fact, God never promises a life without them. Yet we as Christians have developed some odd ideas about how to view God in the midst of difficult, unpredictable seasons. We often think if He doesn't remove the obstacle in front of us, He is not present and walking next to us.

I know this internal struggle personally—the struggle that says, "I should be strong enough to not question God even though my life feels like nothing but one great big question mark." I wholeheartedly understand what it is like to face obstacles that seem endless and insurmountable.

When these difficulties arise, we ultimately have one of two options to choose. One possibility is to stop in our tracks, allowing the overwhelming circumstance to paralyze or stunt any forward motion. The other option is to embrace what we are facing, lean into it, and search for the opportunity hidden inside the obstacle. Although the best choice is clear—to choose to embrace the situation and allow it to help us grow—the reality of walking out that decision is anything but easy. When the unexpected happens, our response is usually to do whatever it takes to gain back whatever we feel we have lost or to make right what we feel is wrong.

Our initial response typically is to not to view this challenge as a learning or growth opportunity. However, when our hearts are open to receive whatever comes our way, we can look at our circumstances through the lens, "What is God trying to teach me through this situation?" He is always speaking to us. He is always leading us to a better way.

As believers, we have access to everything we need through the redemption of our sins in Christ. We can have peace in any situation. We can experience inexplicable joy. We can walk in wisdom and clarity when nothing makes sense. This is the beauty of a relationship with God. No matter what we face, we can be victorious because we are "more than conquerors" in Christ (Romans 8:37). The trials in our life come to temper us and produce spiritual fruit that will remain.

Many Christ-followers spend their lives waiting for God to remove obstacles, change the narrative for them, or move in their current circumstance in a certain way.

The reality is that God uses every single part of our lives, the good and the bad, to cultivate us for His glory. The book of James gives insight on how the trials of life fertilize the godly seeds of character in our lives to perfect our faith (James 1:2–4). If we are always trying to avoid pain and grief, we will forfeit any real growth. We will never mature to our fullest potential as a believer. God ultimately desires for us to grow over the challenging trials life brings.

Joseph Grew Over It

All throughout Scripture, we can see examples of heroes in the faith who had to grow over the difficulties and challenges they faced. Oftentimes, we forget that we are reading these biblical stories knowing the end already, right from the beginning.

Think about it: Daniel had no idea that God would shut up the mouths of the lions, yet he stood his ground in faith. He entered into the den fully acknowledging that he would be walking into a death trap unless God intervened.

The three Hebrew boys—Shadrach, Meshach, and Abednego—had no clue that they would be rescued from the fiery furnace. By refusing to bow to an idol, they accepted death outright and head on, without the knowledge that the Son of God would meet them amidst the fire and deliver them completely unharmed.

Paul was beaten, shipwrecked, and stoned multiple times for sharing the gospel and never knew if he would live to see another day as he traveled from city to city. Yet he persevered and fulfilled the purposes of God for his life, with his testimonies still ringing out to this day.

Joseph is another biblical figure who had to allow God to work in his life as he grew through difficult situations (Genesis 37–47). Jacob gave his son Joseph a multi-colored coat as a sign of his status as the favorite, even though he was the second-youngest. Naturally, Joseph's older brothers resented him.

Now, from time to time, God gave Joseph prophetic dreams and the ability to interpret dreams. Unwisely, when Joseph dreamed that he would prosper over his brothers and they would one day worship him, he scooted right over and told his big brothers about his dream.

The brothers decided they'd had enough. They took Joseph to the wilderness and were prepared to kill him. However, one of Joseph's brothers intervened, and they instead sold him into slavery in Egypt.

But Joseph prospered in his new life. The Bible tells us that by the time he was a young man, Joseph was in charge of his master's entire household. But Joseph, being a good-looking fellow, drew the attention of the mistress of the house, who tried to seduce him. Though Joseph had the good sense to run away, the rejected mistress accused him of attacking her, and Joseph was thrown into prison, falsely accused.

Years went by. Joseph made some allies in jail. He was able to interpret the prophetic dreams two imprisoned servants had, telling these men that one would prosper and the other would be executed. When the servant he'd predicted to prosper was released from jail, he promised to remember Joseph. But more years went by with no word, no change in circumstances.

Eventually, Pharaoh himself began to have disturbing dreams, which no one could interpret. His servant just happened to be the man who'd been in jail with Joseph and suddenly remembered his skill in dream interpretation. Joseph was sent for and told Pharaoh that the dreams meant seven years of plenty were coming, followed by seven years of famine.

Joseph was put in charge of gathering and storing food so Egypt would have enough to get them through the famine. When the famine struck, Joseph's family came from afar to ask for food. Joseph took pity on them and was reconciled to them.

Now, I don't know about you, but if I were in Joseph's shoes, I would have struggled to keep trusting in God through all that. And yet, the Bible tells us that Joseph was faithful. He was so faithful that when his father, Jacob, reflected on Joseph's life from his perspective and with his blessing in Genesis 49:22–24 (NKJV), he said:

> *Joseph is a fruitful bough, a fruitful bough by a well; his branches run over the wall. The archers have bitterly grieved him, shot at him and hated him. But his bow remained in strength, and the arms of his hands were made strong by the hands of the Mighty God of Jacob.*

Whenever Jacob looked back on a life he never really experienced with Joseph, he said of his son, "You are like a vine that grows over the wall." I can just imagine Jacob saying to Joseph, "There is no residue on you!" Joseph didn't give in, get mad, blame his circumstances, or try to fill in gaps that only God could fill with understanding.

Scripture is full of these examples of people who were surrendered fully to the will of the Father and determined to obey, continually growing in grace and godly character as they fulfilled God's purposes for their lives. But how did they have the fortitude to overcome?

Discerning and Prophesying

Like Paul writing to the church of Philippi from a prison cell, we can see the hand of God in every situation. Paul wrote about this perspective in Philippians 1:12: "But I want you to know, brethren, that the things which happened to me have actually turned out for the furtherance of the gospel" (NKJV). Paul was no superhuman, untouchable Christian, but he did tap into something that shaped how he saw his situation, and his response and attitude in the face of persecution. How did he get there? I am convinced it was his *deeply rooted, intimate relationship with God* that allowed him to endure and stay steadfast in the face of such dire circumstances.

The darkest times and most difficult situations will often release you into God-ordained moments, but it takes a discerning spirit to find value in these unexpected places. Discernment to see as God sees flows out of relationship with God. The more intimate our relationship with God, the more peace we have and, oftentimes, the more clarity we can receive for our lives.

It is possible to have this type of relationship; Jesus modeled it for us while still on earth. He told the disciples,

"For I have not spoken on My own authority; but the Father who sent Me gave Me a command, what I should say and what I should speak. And I know that His command is everlasting life. Therefore, whatever I speak, just as the Father has told Me, so I speak" (John 12:49–50 NKJV). The closer we are to the Father, the more rooted we will be in our life and our ability to discern what is actually happening in every circumstance.

Discernment gives us the privilege of thinking with His logic: we can literally have the "mind of Christ" (1 Corinthians 2:16). When we allow the Spirit of God to bring revelation to our situations, we are able to increase our understanding because our viewpoint is now coming from a new place of order and knowledge in God. What a privilege to exercise this type of thinking—to operate with the mind of Christ in every circumstance! His ways are higher and infinitely better than ours could ever be (Isaiah 5:9).

Along those lines, I was recently doing a personal study on prophecy and discovered that prophecy is *not* intended to be about a prophetic voice foretelling someone's future. Rather, prophecy is about each one of us discovering and tapping into the will and message of God in advance so that we may each know which way to go.

In 1 Corinthians 14:1, Paul attested to the importance of this truth when he exhorted the church at Corinth to desire to prophesy. I believe this was not merely about the desire to foretell others' future but also encompassed a person discovering God's will for their own life. It is so important that we each learn to speak the truth and God's purposes over our own lives!

In 1 Corinthians 14:1, "prophesy" is the Greek word *prophēteuō*.[1] This word can mean a few different things, but two meanings that stick out to me in this instance are "foretelling future events pertaining ... to the kingdom of God," and "to utter forth, declare, a thing which can only be known by divine revelation."

You may think this seems unconnected to personal understanding of identity and the will of God for our lives, but I would argue that we have a great example in Matthew 16. When Jesus asked His disciples, "Who do people say the Son of Man is?" (Matthew 16:13), they offered various replies, only to have Jesus ask this pointed follow-up question: "'But what about you,' He asked. 'Who do you say I am?'" It is my impression that this was Jesus' real question the entire time. Of course, we cannot directly know His intention, but we can assume from the many questions Jesus asked that this was a tactic He used to bring further revelation.

Moving on in the dialogue, we see Simon Peter responded to His question by saying, "'You are the Messiah, the Son of the living God.' Jesus replied, 'Blessed are you, Simon son of Jonah, for this was not revealed to you by flesh and blood, but by my Father in heaven. And I tell you that you are Peter, and on this rock I will build my church" (Matthew 16:16–18). Immediately, this curious conversation had turned incredibly revelatory. What started as a discussion of people's opinions soon became a download from heaven. I think we could argue that this fits the definition of *prophesy* as the uttering or declaration of something only knowable by divine revelation.

That is clearly what Peter did at the acknowledgement of Jesus Himself.

Yet the discourse was still not complete with only this piece of the story. Yes, Peter had "tapped in" to a thing that he could only comprehend through the Spirit, but it is the next part that especially encourages me—when Jesus, leaning into this fresh revelation, said to Peter, "And on this rock I will build my church."

Now, we may ask ourselves: Why would Jesus say this to Peter then? Why at that moment? It is my distinct impression that Jesus responded to Peter based on the revelation he had just pronounced. His words come so directly after Peter's that it feels like a natural set-up for us to understand that anything revealed is first about God and then, secondly, about us.

In 1 Corinthians 14, I believe, Paul recognized that many gifts were being sought, possibly without a sense of accountability. But his encouragement to those desiring to be used by God in these special ways was to seek first the revelation that comes through an open spirit to foretell of the kingdom of God. In that place, they would see their own lives revealed so that they might know and do the will of God. In the same way Peter saw and uttered a revealed truth, so Jesus responded with a declaration of identity ("you are Peter") and direction "on this rock I will build my church, and the gates of Hades will not overcome it"). The Corinthians were eager to use their giftings but not as eager to build with them (1 Corinthians 14:12).

I wholeheartedly believe, from my view of Scripture and Jesus' interactions with people, that prophecy as described by Paul in 1 Corinthians 14 is not simply about foretelling a future but about foretelling God's future for us through His Word and His revelation in us. Romans 12:2 tells us not to be conformed to this world, but transformed. How? "By the renewing of your mind. Then you will be able to test and prove what God's will is—his good, pleasing and perfect will." The "will" mentioned in Romans 12:2 means, "what one wishes or has determined shall be done."[2]

So, when Paul wrote to those in Corinth who sought to prophesy, and then to the Romans to "be transformed by the renewing of your mind," he connected two important thoughts. To know God's will for your life, you have to recognize it is not birthed in your own ideas or your own designs. It is not going to come from an article or a personality test. Knowledge of the will of God comes from a transformed mind that has no agenda or expectation of prestige attached, no need for accolades, but simply wants to have the ability to speak something by divine revelation. And I have found that God will never let you know His will for another man until you can understand His will for you.

As we make faith declarations and prophesy to ourselves, we begin to build a greater consciousness of God. As our awareness of God and His will for our lives develops, we begin to understand God's perspective for the world around us and how our life intersects with His ultimate plan. Perspective is God's unique gift to us as humans; He literally enables us to see as He sees. *Wow!*

Scripture gives us many examples of God's willingness to show us His perspective. Matthew 17:1–13, known as the story of the Mount of Transfiguration, comes to mind. This passage from the New Testament shines a light on the personhood of Jesus and helps us understand Him in a deeper way.

In the narrative, Jesus traveled with a few of His close disciples to a mountain of importance in their Jewish tradition. On the mountain, in cooperation with the Father, Jesus was transformed into a radiant light. Then Moses and Elijah appeared in this spectacular, miraculous moment, and the disciples were astounded. Peter immediately asked to build three tabernacles, or tents, to honor them. He intended for the tabernacles to represent these patriarchs of faith who were deeply admired and revered by the Jewish people. They were ambassadors and prophets of the Lord—icons who were vital to the history of the faith.

In the story, as Peter suggested creating these tabernacles, the light of God enveloped them all brilliantly, and the disciples fell facedown to the ground. God's voice suddenly spoke from a cloud saying, "This is my Son, whom I love; with him I am well pleased. Listen to him!" (Matthew 17:5). When they were finally able to look up, Jesus and only Jesus remained on the mountain before them. This is a beautiful depiction of Christ as the Promised One, who fulfills all the prophecies and promises given via the venerable former change agents of the Jewish faith, represented by Moses and Elijah.

Through this magnificent display, Jesus helped His disciples understand something they needed to see firsthand. This picture changed their perspective of who He was and illuminated His role in God's story. Please, do not discount how much perspective matters!

Three Keys to Growing Over It

In my opinion, there are three reasons why the people in these biblical examples were able to do what so many of us fail to do—grow over the wall.

First, they had the right God-view. Joseph, Paul, and many other change agents in Scripture lived with a high consciousness of God in their everyday life. This awareness of God birthed within them an implicit trust. In short, they trusted God. This is such an easy statement to write, and even perhaps read, but living it out is another story! Trust is complicated. It is difficult. It is demanding but rewards us through longevity.

In God's economy, trust is a form of currency. Some may even refer to trust and faith with interchangeable language of intent. Both are built around undeniable hope that the good God we serve is bringing forth good things in our lives. It takes faith to believe God and trust to put your life in His hands.

In Romans 4:18, it is said of Abraham that he hoped "against all hope." Abraham had little apparent reason to keep trusting and hoping for a child. He was a man who had slipped past his fruitful fathering years in the natural and yet was without a child. But God had promised him a child, so he believed anyway. It is amazing what can happen if people just keep believing. I have a friend who once observed, everything good that happens does so because we just keep showing up.

I love when Jesus straight-up asked His disciples, "You do not want to leave too, do you?" (John 6:67). He posed this question to His followers right after experiencing backlash and people bailing on Him. Simon Peter simply answered, "Lord, to whom shall we go? You have the words of eternal life" (John 6:68). Basically, the disciples' attitude was, "We would leave if we hadn't figured out there was such good reason to stay. *You* carry something we do not have, and no one else has, but we know we need!"

All of these patriarchs of the faith knew the intimate reality of what it meant to stay the course and keep believing God. They trusted that God was good and was working on their behalf. They believed that God's plan was the most important thing, even more important than comfort and happiness. When the storm hit, these godly men and women walked through the rain, the wind, the lightning, and the hail, knowing God walked right alongside them.

Secondly, they knew what God thought of them. I have found so often that what creates the most pain in our psyche is not who God is or isn't, but rather the inability to know wholeheartedly what God thinks of us. Because of the vacuum for true spiritual parents in our generation, we have ended up with too many people who are walking with God but still believe that God is ultimately not for them.

This is one of the greatest tragedies I have experienced as a pastor. It is an awful thing to hear someone who you know is a Christ-follower say they are not sure God is for them. Whenever I have been on the receiving end of those words, I have wept in my spirit. It is such a lie—a lie the enemy has fed them and one that has taken root in everything they now see.

Jesus did not come to the earth just to set up a new kingdom or make some religious people mad. He came to redeem mankind. He came to reconcile hearts to Him. In other words, God is so in love with us, He could not bear to spend any additional time without us. He wanted us. He wants *you*!

In Mark 2:1–12, we find a story about a paraplegic. This fellow had a serious need, but he was fortunate to have some crazy, faith-filled friends lower him through a roof to see Jesus. This man was clearly unable to do anything for himself.

Beyond his physical need, he had a much deeper need in his life. In Mark 2:5, Jesus made this statement: "Son, your sins are forgiven you" (NKJV). Jesus accepted the paraplegic man before He healed him. Why? Ultimately, this man was not just in need of a physical miracle but an emotional and spiritual one, too. Jesus desired to heal his emotional life before He healed his physical life.

In Jewish culture of the day, it was common to care for your loved ones as a family when they were unable to care for themselves.[3] Clearly, from the context of the story, this man was living all alone without such support. Jesus saw that and determined what this man needed was not just a redeemed body but also a reconciled relationship, a way back to where he belonged. Accordingly, I believe the reason Jesus then told him, "Go home," was that He knew the man needed to return to the people who had rejected him, to forgive them just as Jesus had forgiven him.

This story summarizes the entire mission of Jesus. He came to redeem us so that we could return to His family, where we all belong. Through Him, we are no longer slaves; we can walk in our proper identity as sons and daughters of the Most High God. When we have the right perspective regarding what God thinks of us, we know that we are not alone. We belong to the family of God.

Do you know that hell's primary attribute is separation from God? When we do not live in the knowledge of what God thinks of us, we end up living in hellish conditions emotionally without even realizing it! We live beneath the benefits and belonging that Jesus died to give us. God is always working on our behalf because we are His precious, beloved children.

If you want to know what God thinks about you, get into the Word of God. The Scriptures operate like a mirror for our hearts and minds. Each time we look into that mirror, the Word, we are being transformed into the image of Christ by the Spirit of the Lord (2 Corinthians 3:18). This transformation is not just about shaping our identity in Christ but also about God's identity in us. That doesn't mean everything will be easy, but it does mean God is always in control. He will do what is best for His child.

Finally, they thought rightly about their situations. Joseph, Paul, Daniel, and many others in Scripture experienced heartbreak, betrayal, suffering, and brokenness. They recognized that suffering and pain are a part of life. We all experience pain. We all are broken. Yet these biblical examples had the right perspective and, in spite of it all, lived their lives based on what God revealed to them.

God is always able to work a situation for our good and His glory.

Too often, when we encounter situations that are contrary to our desired future, we forget God's heart for us and take the reins in our own hands. We put our trust in our own abilities, we succumb to the opinions of others, or we decide it is simply too hard and give up all together. We feel like we can only trust God if He removes the wall in front of us, instead of helping us grow over it. But when we consciously put our focus on God's thoughts about us and trust Him completely, we can overcome and live victoriously.

God ultimately knows the best circumstances, the best soil, that will produce the best in us and for us. We have to rely on His pruning and continue to sow the seeds of the Word into our hearts.

In this book, we will explore how you can align your perspective with God's perspective in a way that will help you grow over the walls in your life. I hope you read this book and walk away with the realization that God has great plans for you. He has a dream for you and will be there every moment, even when you come up against a mighty wall. Will you give up or grow over it?

CHAPTER ONE

Dreaming God-Given Dreams

> *In the last days, God says, I will pour out my Spirit on all people. Your sons and daughters will prophesy, your young men will see visions, your old men will dream dreams.*
> —*Acts 2:17* NIV

Joseph was called a dreamer by his older brothers, and they didn't mean it as a compliment. In fact, in the very next verse, they plotted to kill him (Genesis 37:19–20). Take a moment and read Genesis chapter 37 in its entirety. Here, we see a seventeen-year-old Joseph—who was the apple of his father's eye—tattling on his older brothers. His father, Jacob (or Israel) gave Joseph a special robe that clearly showed the world he was his father's favorite.

And then Joseph had some prophetic dreams. It's clear that those dreams showed Joseph would one day be the ruler over his brothers. Between the tattling, the coat, and the dreams, his older brothers got pretty steamed.

Now, I don't know whether or not God told Joseph to tell his dream to his brothers. It seems foolhardy to me. I can easily picture young, handsome Joseph searching out his big brothers and bragging, "Hey, guys! Guess what dream God gave me!" But whether or not God told him to tell his dream, it sure caused some big problems for Joseph.

I find it interesting that in verses 14 to 17, Joseph tried to track down his brothers who kept hiding from him. I have three kids, and there have certainly been times when the two older ones didn't want to play with the youngest. These verses remind me of that. Picture those ten older brothers hearing that Joseph was on the way, picking up their stuff, and hurrying to get away, grumbling the whole way.

They were angry enough by the time Joseph tracked them down to want to kill him! Reuben, though, convinced the brothers not to kill Joseph but to sell him into slavery. Talk about a major obstacle to overcome!

Vain Dreams vs. God-Given Dreams

When we come to Christ and have our Pentecost moment, in which the Holy Spirit becomes a part of our lives, we start on a path toward God's big dream for us. This dream involves our talents, our experiences, and our natural gifting. It is all about advancing God's kingdom and making an eternal impact.

Unfortunately, it's easy to get it all wrong. You see, we modern Christians are lovers of vain dreams. We dream of things that will make us look better to those around us, make us more comfortable, or get us lots of praise.

Sometimes we pretend our vain dreams are selfless, but

at the core they are entirely selfish. We try to convince ourselves that we only want the very best vacation Bible school this town has ever seen in order to win kids to Jesus, when really we want to show up the snooty church across town. We sing in the choir in order to get recognized as a great soloist; we preach sermons in order to get pats on the back for our brilliance; we go on a mission trip to prove how holy we are.

In reality, any dream God gives you should be scary. Scary as in, there is absolutely no way that it can ever happen in your own strength and ability. A God-given dream is one that can only come from the Holy Spirit and be accomplished by the power of the Holy Spirit at work in our lives. These dreams are prophetic in nature.

No God-given dream is a walk in the park or comes with a well-known, step-by-step plan of execution. Most God-given dreams feel a bit confusing and can even be misunderstood in the beginning stages. I think this happened with Joseph.

I believe Joseph had a prophetic insight about his future, but because he didn't understand it, he misappropriated it. He disclosed his dream to the wrong people at the wrong time. Although dreams are prophetic in nature, they must be discerned in practice.

Let me give you some qualifications for a God-given dream.

First, every God-given dream is birthed in the Spirit. In other words, it is not just your great idea. It is really a God idea. There is a difference. Joseph was given the dreams from God—they were not his original thought! His prophetic dreams ended up causing him more problems than he would have liked, I am sure. His dreams also pointed to God's provision and intervention—to a greater purpose than just benefiting Joseph personally. They were a foretelling of how God would help provide for His people during difficult times, through Joseph's life.

A dream birthed in the Spirit means it has been bathed in prayer and mirrored against the character and nature of God in the Word, and is always beyond your own thinking. Whenever I feel like God has given me a download from heaven as a dream in my heart, I first and foremost take it to prayer. I know this may sound quite simple, but I have a lot of dreams and it takes diligence to allow my dreams to be processed in my prayer life.

Sometimes this means journaling my thoughts on a dream based on my time with God, while other times it means stirring myself up in faith to believe this is possible and that it could be a piece of the future I am intended to contend for. My father always says a dream given by God is "God's preferred future" over our lives. In order to discover if this is God's preferred future, we have to pray into it.

My mother has been an important voice in my life. One of the many things I admire about her is her tenacity to believe for something that feels out of reach. From my early days as a child into my adulthood, I have watched firsthand her diligence to process God dreams and pull them into reality. Whether it was her desire to own her own home or starting a citywide feeding ministry, she has always been a woman of prayer. She is passionate about prayer and often discusses the concerning lack of prayer in the body of Christ today.

We live in such a fast-paced, self-serve culture that sometimes prayer feels pointless or slow. However, I have found that prayer is central in processing my dreams, ideas, and plans. Anytime I have taken time to inquire of the Lord in prayer, I have never been disappointed. God always responds. He is never distant. I just have to continue to take my dreams and ideas and everything in my life to Him in my quiet times of prayer and devotion.

Secondly, a God-given dream demands partnership. God never intended for us to do life alone. With Joseph's dreams, although he did not yet understand fully, his family would benefit from his obedience. He would also partner with Pharaoh, as the Egyptian ruler's second-in-command, to bring blessing and provision to Joseph's family and his nation. This was not possible without partnership and relationships. Thus, no God-given dream will be a "stand alone" dream. It will always demand partnership to benefit and build up the kingdom of God, who works best in these partnerships.

In the New Testament, Jesus released His disciples two by two to share the gospel together everywhere they traveled. When Peter caught more fish than his nets could handle, he called for his partners, fisherman nearby, to help pull in the abundant catch. When God created mankind, He knew it was not beneficial for man to tend the earth, populate it, and take dominion alone.

One of my favorite people, Dan Rockwell, once said, "Learn to build relationships before you need them." What a statement of truth in life and particularly in dreaming God dreams. Partnership is part of a God dream.

I was once in a meeting with Bill Johnson and heard him say, "Whenever God favors us, it has to benefit others or it was misused favor."[4] It reminds me of the statement the Queen of Sheba made to King Solomon in 1 Kings 10:9 "Blessed be Jehovah thy God [who was delighted to] set thee on the throne of Israel: because Jehovah loved Israel for ever" (ASV). In other words, Solomon was favored so that he could extend his favor to God's people through righteous governance. God dreams never just benefit the dreamer.

Dreams go beyond us into ministering the purposes of God through us. Joseph did not understand the full meaning of his earlier dreams, with his family bowing down to him. After being betrayed and left for dead by his own brothers, enduring prison, and rising to power as the second-in-command in Egypt under Pharoah, Joseph fulfilled his prophetic destiny of delivering his family from famine. He was able to extend favor to the very ones who had caused him great harm and heartache. Joseph could see in that moment with his brothers, God had used every event in his life to lead him to a place of redemption.

I can still remember the first time I was invited to speak in Uganda. A man walked up to me at a conference and asked for my email. Against my better judgment (or so I thought), I obliged.

Later that evening, I received an email asking me if I would come to Africa and bring the word of the Lord. Six months earlier, I had received a prophetic awakening word, which sent me to my prayer closet. This word centered on the central theme that the world was opening to me but to be aware and discerning of these opportunities.

The direction given in this specific prophetic word was that I would know the right doors for me based on the language used—the literal words of invitation given.

When I received the email that night, the man writing the email repeated back to me verbatim the words the prophet had told me to be looking for. In an instant, I knew I was supposed to go. That was eight years ago. Today, what began as a two-hundred-member pastor meeting has grown into a training and church-planting school with 1,500 pastors in attendance. In addition, over the course of those eight years, this ministry completed their church building that seats over a thousand people, a remarkable feat for the impoverished area where these meetings are held. All of this came to be due to the catalyst of a God-given dream.

God longs to deposit His dreams in your heart as well. You might have an actual dream in your sleep; you might have a burning desire in your heart that won't go away; or maybe someone speaks prophetically into you and it bears witness to your spirit. Any of these is possible, and these methods can sometimes occur simultaneously.

Some dreams are seasonal, having a specific timeframe, while other dreams can take a lifetime to accomplish. As a child, you might start thinking about something, and as you grow to a teenager, you continue to feel the tug to take this path or follow this direction.

God's dreams for us can require years of training, or even years of hardship, that shape us into who He needs us to be to fulfill His dream for our lives. Don't be discouraged if that is the case! God is so faithful. He never gives us dreams to tease us or create disappointment. He is the Giver and ultimate Fulfiller of Dreams!

Share Your Dreams with Discretion

Once I was riding in a car with a close friend and we were in deep discussion about our futures. I love these types of conversations—sharing passionately and yet in a safe space with a friend. However, when I began to share about some things I saw over my future, and over global leadership in the world, something clearly shifted in the discussion.

The more I shared my thoughts, the quieter the car got until I realized I had left my companion behind miles ago mentally, though they were still physically there in the car with me. At first, I started to back up from my bold declarations and musings, but then I decided, *"If she doesn't get it, that's okay, but I am going to share my thoughts and dream anyway."*

Many months went by, and one day this same friend was in a conversation with some other leaders when she began to share my "crazy" thoughts openly and without regard. I knew these dreams and ideas were still being developed when I shared them with her privately. I had no idea she would openly share them as concrete and solidified. As you can guess, the end result was me answering more questions than I was ready for, and some leaders walking away thinking I was insane and my ideas foolish.

There are times when you might be tempted to share your God-given dream to anyone who sits still enough to listen. Much like Joseph, we get excited about what the

Lord shows us and foolishly share with those who are not prepared to receive it, or who will respond out of jealousy or spite. Let me suggest that a mature Christian realizes that not every audience is the right audience. Sometimes close friends are not even the right environment.

Dreams are like eggs of purpose and need to be incubated in the right environments and hearts. Believers who can handle the dreams of another are mature in Spirit, have clear identity about who they are, and do not think of you as a threat. For me, this has been spiritual men and women who I knew could have skin in the game without having to take over the game. They are voices who guide, inquire, direct, and build.

God-given dreams are not an acquisition. They are discovered, processed, and executed over time. Many times, these dreams are so big that they are actually quite scary! You might find you are reluctant to share the dream God has given you because that makes it more real. But what God births He will bring forth if you let Him.

My dad had a picture hanging in his office for years that said, "The will of God will never lead you where the grace of God cannot keep you." God-given dreams will always be bigger than you anticipate, but do not be intimidated or scared because of the size of your dream. The dream is big, but you serve a *big* God. He will do what He says He will do! It's about God, and He will bring it to fruition in His time.

Walk Out the Process

God delights in the process far more than He delights in the outcomes. This means that the process of how we handle opportunity, dreams, and ideas matters to God. Remember the Parable of the Talents in Matthew 25? The servant who hid his talent for safekeeping was described as a "wicked and lazy servant" by the master. Why? Because he did nothing with what had been put into his hands.

God is always looking for people who are willing to walk out the process and do something with what He puts into our hands. The parable explains that in God's economy, it is better to use what God gives you and embrace the possibility of making a mistake, versus inaction and burying what has been given to you.

God is big enough to cover our mishaps. He is gracious enough to help us overcome our own fears and doubts to step out in faith and accomplish the dreams He places in our hearts.

Joseph's Obstacle: People's Opinions

Joseph's brothers were angered by the dream God gave him. They were already irritated by him, and this latest incident (sharing his dream that elevated his status above his family) was the proverbial straw that broke the camel's back. They decided that if they got rid of Joseph, this dream would never come to pass.

We face similar obstacles in our own lives, don't we? We step out in faith to walk toward God's plan, and things happen. It doesn't take long before the people around us start offering their opinions, and it is very tempting to let naysayers stop us from growing in the way God intended.

I always knew God wanted me to be a preacher. However, when I was twenty-years old and just one year from graduating college, I became pregnant without being married. My parents were loving and supportive, but there were plenty of others who were not. People started to talk about how it was too bad that my future as a preacher was never going to happen now that I'd messed up.

But my mistakes didn't change God's plan for my life. The actions of Joseph's brothers didn't change God's plans, either. Don't allow the voices and words of people around you to become more important than what God has put in your heart.

People are all too glad to tell you limitations exist. Some of those limitations are real, and some are imagined. Consider the voices and opinions you allow to influence your life. Learn to test the walls, knock down the false ones, and then let God show you how to grow over the real obstacles on the way to fulfilling your God-given purpose.

Remember, obstacles are a sure thing, an absolute in life's journey. Joseph faced some terrible obstacles: betrayal, imprisonment, temptation. Don't be surprised when hardships block your path. Instead, run to God and put your hand firmly in His, trusting that He will use these hardships in big ways in your life.

Joseph was a beloved son even in captivity and in prison. That never changed. You are a beloved, wanted, adopted child of God. When others tear you down, you remain a beloved child of God. When you make huge mistakes, you are still a beloved child of God.

If God has called you to do something, you'd better believe that He will prepare you for it. God has depths of strength, wisdom, courage, and ability that you cannot imagine. Accept help when offered, but don't let your fear be louder than the voice of your Heavenly Father calling you to greatness.

WORKBOOK

Chapter One Questions

Do I trust God in this? What is it that God is calling you to do? What is the dream that's been flickering in your heart of hearts? Now, what obstacles exist around that dream? Where have you been trusting God to make that dream come true in His time, and where have you been doubting His goodness?

_____

_____

_____

_____

_____

_____

_____

_____

Who does God say I am? Do you feel too small, too insignificant, or too ill-equipped to carry out the dream God has given you? What does God say about this?

_____

_____

_____

_____

_____

_____

_____

Who do I say I am? Is your declaration over yourself in alignment with who God has called you to be?

_____

_____

_____

_____

_____

_____

_____

Chapter One Notes

CHAPTER TWO

Are You Abiding?

Abide in Me, and I in you. As the branch cannot bear fruit of itself, unless it abides in the vine, neither can you, unless you abide in Me.

I am the vine, you are the branches. He who abides in Me, and I in him, bears much fruit; for without Me you can do nothing.

—*John 15:4–5 NKJV*

As a culture, we have lost the ability to abide well. We are impatient. We are quick to get out. We want instant gratification. People hop from church to church, from job to job, from friendship to friendship, sometimes with good reasons and sometimes just on a whim.

It's no wonder, then, that we really struggle with the concept of abiding in God. It takes work to learn to listen to Him. Sometimes God is silent when we really want Him to speak to us about a specific decision or desired outcome. We have to learn how to wait on the Lord and seek His face. We must humble ourselves and submit our desires to His leadership.

Abiding in Christ means that we are actively cultivating a deeper relationship with our Savior. Some folks describe it as seeking His face and not just His hand. Abiding means that you learn to enjoy His presence without always having an agenda. So often, we just want to skip to the part where we're showing off the fabulous fruit we've produced.

The problem is that we don't always recognize good fruit when we see it. Galatians 5:22–23 describes the fruit we should see in our life as a follower of Christ—the fruit of "love, joy, peace, patience, kindness, goodness, faithfulness, gentleness, and self-control" (NLT). In our Christian culture, particularly, we tend to misread gifting for fruit.

First, let me say, God has given each one of us a gift. It is the beautiful working of God in us. But gifts are never a good indication of fruitfulness, because they are just that—gifts. A gift always says more about the giver than the recipient.

If I were to give someone who was living on the streets a Mercedes tomorrow, does it make that person any different? Not really. They may still be living on the streets, just driving a Mercedes without a home or job or bed.

The giver is the one who gets the glory of the gift because it says more about them and their generosity than the worthiness of the recipient. This is often misunderstood in our culture. We believe that gifts are interchangeable for fruit. This is why we can start following someone on social media, and read and repost their thoughts, without ever considering what their character is like behind the post and social media persona. It is possible they are simply a gifted communicator who is terribly inconsistent or unkind in real life.

First and foremost, we must reassess how we are determining fruitfulness. The Bible is abundantly clear on this matter. The apostle Paul, who wrote over half of the New Testament,[5] confronted the "gift versus fruit" issue, often and especially in the church at Corinth. It was Corinthians who excelled in giftedness and talent but rarely lived fruitfully.[6]

Fruitfulness is developed one way—through relationship. Any true fruit in the Kingdom is connected to the King. In the New Testament, Jesus made life with Him clear: if you want to be fruitful, you live connected to the vine. When you are connected to the vine, fruit is the by-product.

Paul gave us a description of different fruits that are always being developed in us as Christ-followers. He talked about patience, love, longsuffering, and joy being fruits of the Spirit. These fruits are all characteristics of the Holy Spirit. As we are in relationship with the Holy Spirit, we develop His character, which is Jesus' lifestyle and character. This means we cannot discount the ongoing relationship we are to have with the Holy Spirit.

We can observe this evidence in others as well. A life walking with the Holy Spirit has some important, recognizable distinctions. One such distinction is selflessness. The Holy Spirit is never self-serving. In fact, Jesus described the Holy Spirit by explaining that the Spirit will demonstrate this godly life in us and will always point to and speak of Jesus (John 14:26).

Selfishness withholds goodness and barricades love when it feels like it, but selflessness is always working to "love your neighbor as yourself" (Mark 12:31 NKJV). When I am observing people's lives, I am always looking for people who are unloading goodness on others. They freely give because they have freely received.

There is a well-known story in the Bible about an Old Testament prophet, Jonah, who was ultimately called to bring God's message of forgiveness to his enemies, the people of Nineveh. Through a series of events, stubborn Jonah ended up in the belly of a whale. Eventually, Jonah got to Nineveh and shared God's forgiveness with his enemies in fulfillment of God's assignment for his life.

When we look at this story, it is important that we see Jonah as God saw him. I believe Jonah had an incredible understanding of the goodness and nature of God. Jonah knew God was so good and so rich in mercy, he did not want to go to Nineveh because he simply could not bear to see the character of God play out (Jonah 4:2). So he fought God every step of the way.

The real sin for Jonah was not his choice of transportation or even his basic unwillingness to go, but his selfishness. He could not bear for God to forgive the people he hated. Therefore, Jonah worked desperately to withhold the goodness of God from the people He was trying to send it to, through Jonah.

We all have Ninevehs in our lives—people who have wronged us and places where we have been wronged. God uses the willingness in our hearts to obey Him unselfishly to display His character and His goodness to those very people and in those specific situations. Our relationship with the Holy Spirit shapes this willing and selfless obedience.

When we are looking for fruit on display, not only do we look for a selfless life but we also look for a joyful life. People walking with God should be joyful because there is joy in the Holy Spirit. If I am around people who look like they just sucked on a lemon, I want to run around the fence post, pulling my hair out. There is nothing more discouraging than being with Christ-followers who refuse to live in joy. Part of finding healthy fruit in us and around us is to keep our joy meter up.

The Bible finds joy so important to our walk with God, it is written in Nehemiah 8:10 that "the joy of the LORD is your strength" (NIV). There is strength in joy. This tells me some people are worn out not because of a devil or wall in front of them but because their joy bucket is low. We fill up our joy bucket, first, through relationship with God and, secondly, through serving other people.

I love how Donald Clifton describes this principle of sharing goodness in his theory of the dipper and the bucket.[7] He explains what it means to fill up and distribute out from our lives. The key principle he shares is that life is ultimately fulfilling based on how we are treated or how we treat others.

As Christ-followers, we can know that hardships are inevitable, to be misunderstood will be an unavoidable occurrence, but we can overcome. Clifton's premise suggests that our lives are buckets to be filled and emptied, which correlates with a biblical understanding of life.

If we are to have the strength to grow over hardships in our paths, we must learn to abide well. We must allow the

Holy Spirit to fill us up daily so we can pour out God's goodness to those we interact with each day. We will have the strength to push through difficult spaces, to overcome those seemingly impossible walls and grow over challenges into the person God intends for us to be, fulfilling His special purpose for us.

The Trouble with Abiding

If abiding in God has all these benefits, why do we struggle?

When I was in Napa Valley a few years ago, I had the privilege of taking a property tour of one of the vineyards. I love to educate myself with new facts, and this type of tour was right up my "inquisitive mind needs to know" alley. While I was on the tour, I observed the vinedresser methodically trimming back leaves, tucking in rogue branches, and pushing dirt around the vine root system. He would check fence posts and straighten wires, all while telling us about the grapes, the history of the vineyard, and the care needed for it. While I listened and observed, I became increasingly interested in why he was doing some of the things he was seemingly absentmindedly doing.

Apparently, I was not alone in this, as moments later, one of the other tourists spoke up and asked, "Sir, why are you tucking the branches back into the other branches in that twisting motion?" With the sweat running down his forehead, clearly in his element and field of expertise, the vinedresser answered, "I tuck the lone branches into others, and I twist them, to make room for more fruit." He went on to explain that the vine gave the branches life but one branch alone could not produce a sizable harvest. When the branches collectively were tucked into one another, they could handle and produce more fruit.

In that moment, I was struck with this picture and revelatory thought: abiding in God, in John 15, is so much more than just a basic picture of relationship. It is a deep illustration of life with God and with others.

To grasp fully what it means to abide in the vine of Christ, we have to unpack this passage, in which Jesus spoke to us not only about the relationship of man to God but also about the relationship between the Father and Jesus. In John 15:9–10, Jesus said, "As the Father loved Me, I have also loved you; abide in My love. If you keep My commandments, you will abide in My love, just as I have kept My Father's commandments and abide in His love" (NKJV). We see here the correlation between believers, Jesus, and the Father as an ongoing relationship of abiding love and submission.

This passage of Scripture is so important because it reveals trusted, submitted relationship. We often try desperately to avoid and never speak about this type of submission. Jesus openly and confidently helped us see in John 15 that abiding in Him does not just involve our trust and submission to Him but also includes Jesus' own submission to the Father as a covering and caretaker.

The Father is the Vinedresser, the one who ultimately determines the care and activity of the vine and branches. Just like the vinedresser on the day of my tour so carefully trimmed and tucked while describing his beautiful vineyard oasis, so the Father does the same for us when we hide ourselves in the nature and ways of Christ.

Abiding is complicated. It is difficult because it demands willing submission to the way of the vine. It demands submission to Christ, His ways, His will, His growth strategy. I have honestly struggled at times to give up control in the way that is necessary for an abiding life. Submission is not a new word or a new way of living, but it is misunderstood in many circles. First of all, the Bible is full of submission language. It is a gospel of freedom; however, it is a gospel that gives us the freedom to submit. When Paul wrote that we are "free in Christ" (Galatians 5:13), he was not writing about our freedom to live as we desire but instead was pinpointing the freedom we ultimately have to serve one another lovingly and "to become children of God," as John so keenly wrote (John 1:12).

God has given us the power to *become*. When we live a surrendered life, the Spirit of God sets us free to become sons and daughters, to become the people God intended us to be on the earth. To utilize this power, we have to learn to abide in complete submission to God.

We have to give up control. Staying in control is a central theme for many of us. It is also the leading cause of our misery, our weariness, and our unhealthy attachments.

Steve Maraboli states in his book, *Unapologetically You,* "The reason many people in our society are miserable, sick, and highly stressed is because of unhealthy attachment to things they have no control over."[8] As Christ-followers, we have to reconcile our control issues with God's sovereignty. This means that even though we desperately want to remain in control, we recognize that to try to do so will only impede us in placing God first in our lives.

It is impossible to say we trust God and desire for Him to lead our lives yet simultaneously try to stay in control of every aspect of our lives. It is pointless to turn over control to God but then continue to plot and plan our lives out of the same limited perceptions and understandings as before.

When we decide to abide in God, we give up a lot of control over our lives. Jesus told His disciples in John 6:54, "He who eats My flesh and drinks My blood has eternal life" (NASB). Jesus was giving His listeners the strategy of relationship with Him.

Like with many of Jesus' words, the listening crowd was more offended by His lessons than transformed. Jesus was not saying people had to literally eat His body and drink His blood; rather, He wanted them to understand symbolically that it is a deep work of both consuming His Word and drinking in His new wine with abandonment— embracing His work on the cross completely—that causes this great abiding to take place. In order to abide in Him, we cannot retain control. It requires a turning over to His will and His ways.

The struggles of all mankind are summed up in just a few questions, one of which is simply, "Who is in control?" Maybe the question to ask is, "What does it look like for me to take off the crown of control in my life and lean into abiding differently in Him?" We may start to hear the Holy Spirit's promptings differently.

When He tells us to go here or there, to spend our time or money in these ways, and to respond to problems patiently, we choose to obey and do not fight back with questions or concerns about, additions to, or subtractions from the Word. This level of submission and complete obedience can be a scary, hard thing, but it is truly the only way to abide.

In reality, this is where we must come face to face with our true beliefs about God's trustworthiness. Do I really believe that He has my best interest at heart? Do I trust that He is going to walk with me through hardship and give my suffering good purposes? Do I honestly think that my time on earth is temporary and the Kingdom is eternal?

We like telling God our plans and ideas for our lives. For example, we may want to be an apple tree. We are not happy at all when He tells us that He created us to be a grapevine instead. "No, God, I wanted to be a great singer. No, God, I wanted to be a millionaire. No, God, I wanted to be married with children by the age of thirty-five."

Listen—God is so good! He has wonderful gifts and is able to achieve purposes you never dreamed! When we truly begin to trust Him, we surrender our own plans, hopes, and dreams to His divine design. You have to learn to abide and trust Him in order to experience the full beauty of those plans.

Abiding requires maturity. Maturity is taking the high road, not being easily offended, and living with a growth mindset that says you are responsible for your actions and choices. Simply put, being a victim excuses us from taking responsibility. It's someone else's fault, not mine.

Victim-mentality Christians only produce rotten fruit. It is never healthy or strong or nourishing. Living on a steady diet of a victim mentality is like living off a diet of deep-fried Twinkies. It might feel good going down, but it won't feel good later and it absolutely will never make us into healthy, growing people.

When we abide in Christ, we learn two important lessons. The first lesson is that God is sovereign. He is in charge of everything. He will take every mistake, every moment of suffering, and every wrong done to us and use it for His eternal purposes. Therefore, we get to rejoice when hardship happens because God has more material to work with.

Secondly, when we abide, we are responsible for confessing and repenting of our sin and working to walk in obedience. We are not a victim of our sin; we are the perpetrators of our sin. We must address it in order to grow strong vines that can handle life's obstacles. This is maturity.

Abiding requires long, hard, disciplined work. Abiding in God doesn't happen easily. You don't get saved, experience the Holy Spirit, and suddenly know what to do in every situation. Putting on a "What Would Jesus Do?" bracelet doesn't mean you know the answer to that question. We grow in our faith through *spiritual disciplines.* We must train ourselves to spend time with God by reading His Word and praying. We must learn how to hear the Holy Spirit. Tithing, fasting, loving our neighbors, confessing and repenting of sin—all of these things come with time, practice, and patience.

Let's go back to the picture of the vine. Plants require a lot of work. Beautiful, healthy gardens need careful planning and tending. If a gardener plants a vine, he must prepare the soil, water the plant, add fertilizer, trim it, and keep the weeds at bay. Encouraging a vine to climb a fence takes careful placement. The gardener has to keep the vine growing in the right direction. He keeps a check on the progress of what is growing in his garden each day. He knows he can make his garden flourish by using certain methods and techniques. The gardener is *intentional*.

Do you feel you aren't growing spiritually? Are you putting in the work?

God is so gracious and compassionate. He is waiting patiently to help us tend our own gardens—our souls. We can come to Him and give Him the soil of our heart, no matter the state, and He is so faithful to gently guide us into cultivating a thriving vine.

Spending time in prayer, reading the Word daily, taking time to journal and reflect, allowing the Holy Spirit to speak to your heart—these are some of the disciplines that will produce an abundant, healthy soul with spiritual fruit that remains. We are as close to God as *we* choose to be. He is ever-present, waiting for us to come to Him.

WORKBOOK

Chapter Two Questions

Do I trust God in this? Where is abiding difficult for you? Do you feel that you are leaning heavily on your gifts rather than challenging yourself to chase God's plans in ways where you aren't naturally gifted?

_____
_____
_____
_____
_____
_____
_____
_____
_____
_____
_____

Who does God say I am? What are your gifts—spiritual and otherwise? Which spiritual disciplines come easily for you? Which are harder?

_____
_____
_____
_____
_____
_____
_____
_____
_____

Who do I say I am? What do you need to do in order to better abide with God? Create a plan for how you will take a step forward in at least one spiritual discipline this week.

_____
_____
_____
_____
_____
_____

_____

_____

_____

_____

Chapter Two Notes

CHAPTER THREE

Taking Off Emotional Armor

I love to travel and am fortunate to have the privilege of traveling often for various reasons. One of my favorite places to visit is the Tower of London in London, England.

Because of my passion for history, I always enjoy visiting historical locations to see what was happening during that time period and what it might have been like to live during that part of history. (At the same time, I am always thankful that I live in this place and time!)

Whenever I visit, I cannot miss seeing the Line of Kings at the Tower of London. The Line of Kings displays the armor of famous kings of England. As I walk through the displayed galleries, I am always overwhelmed with the reality of the weight of the royal armor.

Many of these suits of armor, although designed to protect a wearer, would hold their shape even standing alone, without a person inside. The armor takes the shape of the man it was made for. What an incredible work by the artisans of that day!

Obviously, we no longer use this type of armor in today's world, yet many people live with their own set of armor as if they were kings of fifteenth-century England. Just like the armor of historical kings, this type of armor is also made to fit the one it protects. This armor is emotional, psychological, and sometimes a conscious protective mechanism that we use to shield ourselves from pain, hurt, disappointment, and disillusionment.

Our armor is primarily emotionally driven. It is almost always in response to something that we did not see coming or an outcome we could not understand. Emotional armor is the result of emotional wounds. These unhealed wounds often leave us feeling vulnerable in ways we do not want and exposed to things we desire to be protected from. We can subconsciously develop these protective barriers in our lives to the point that they remain in place all the time, holding their shape like the "stand alone" armor in the Tower of London.

Unlike physical armor that protects you from an exterior enemy, emotional armor is dangerous and harmful to the person wearing it. First, emotional armor quickly becomes a daily necessity for your psyche. Once you learn to carry the weight of armor, you struggle to get rid of that weight. It feels comforting and necessary but it is really damaging and defeating.

Recently, my daughter was given a weighted blanket. These blankets are created with weights sewn into the lining so that the extra weight will help those who suffer with anxiety by providing a calming, swaddling feeling, according to a Harvard Health Publishing article from 2019.[9] In other words, the weighted sensation creates a feeling of safety and comfort. Much like a weighted blanket, emotional armor gives a false sense of comfort. You begin to feel safer with the walls you have created in your heart and mind.

Secondly, emotional armor is dangerous because it creates and sustains unhealthy mindsets. Mindsets are important because they set the course for your life. Just because a thought enters your mind does not mean it is true. Our personally designed emotional armor gets in the way of thinking clearly, and as a result, we end up believing thoughts that do not line up with the truth. Second Corinthians 10:5 says that we overcome when we "capture every thought and make it obey Christ" (EXB). We can so idolize our opinion of a situation that we no longer subject our thoughts to any other input. Emotional armor may keep bad things out, but it also keeps good things from coming in.

Thirdly, emotional armor restricts growth. The title of this book is *Grow Over It!*, so it would be remiss of me not to lean into the reality that the unhealthy patterns we create for ourselves actually restrict our lives. This armor protects us, but it also restricts our growth.

The protection mechanisms we create often make us critical of others and cynical toward anything that is healthy and growing. No one grows with critical behavior or cynical worldviews of others. *Stagnation* means "the state of not flowing or moving."[10] When you wear your emotional armor front and center, you block the flow of God in you and through you. You can never fully grow behind armor because the energy needed to grow is put toward carrying the weight around. There are three primary causes in life that produce this practice of wearing emotional armor: offense, rejection, and weariness.

Offense

There is a great story in the Bible about a man named Gideon who did some incredible things for God, including conquering an entire army with only three hundred men. However, one issue that haunted Gideon's life was his unwillingness to get over offense.

When Gideon went to Ephraim, his neighboring brothers, for help in the battle of his life, they refused to help. They never saw the potential Gideon saw and refused to fight alongside him. This must have deeply offended Gideon. Not only did they refuse to go to battle with him, but they had no confidence in his efforts. Gideon probably already had a bit of insecurity since he was from the least tribe of Israel and carried no significant ranking.

I can only imagine how hurtful it was for Gideon to realize his neighbors were not willing to help him. It appears that Gideon never really forgot his Ephraimite brothers' actions. Following the battle and victory, Gideon used the spoils to makes his own ephod. This is interesting because the leaders of Israel would come to Shiloh, which was in the land of Ephraim, to use the ephod of Israel in ceremonies to seek the Lord.[11]

Why would Gideon create his own ephod? Why not just take the gold and create something else? Some commentaries suggest that it was an effort "to keep some direct hold on the nation's worship."[12] I tend to believe that Gideon created his own ephod to ensure that he would never have to return to Ephraim.

Perhaps Gideon had not dealt with the offense in his heart toward the brothers who left him to go to battle alone. Out of self-defense in his own heart, he found a way to make sure his worship was never dependent upon their location again. Let's imagine this was the case and Gideon wanted to ensure that his brothers knew he was not dependent on them for anything.

The Bible says in Judges 8:27, "And all Israel played the harlot with it [the ephod] there. It became a snare to Gideon and to his house" (NKJV). An ephod was a garment worn by certain prophets and priests as they sought the Lord for direction in the Old Testament.[13] It was used by Samuel, David, and many others in the history of Israel. Could it be that Gideon was so fueled by an offense that he literally created a new strategy of worship to God so he would never have to interact with his brothers again?

This situation certainly translates to today. How many people do you know who have left a church, a job, or a friendship simply because they got offended? Their offense led them to create a new way to get where they wanted to go. Unfortunately, each time we make up new ways to relate to God or one another, we create space in our lives, our families, and our futures for the enemy to gain a foothold.

Gideon had been a very successful leader, but he may not have been a successful man. Gideon and his family were deeply affected by this choice to live in offense. Proverbs 18:19 says that "a brother offended is harder to win than a strong city" (NKJV).

In order to drop the armor that surrounds offense, we have to do the opposite of what Gideon did. We have to forgive instead of grow bitter. We have to seek to repair the breach and remove the obstacles in our way instead of avoiding the blockage and building bypasses around it. The Bible gives clear instructions as to what to do when offense comes to our lives: we go to the brother or sister who has offended us and work to bring resolution to the relationship (Matthew 5:23–24; Matthew 18:15–20).

When we refuse to follow this path of biblical reconciliation, we allow the offender to live rent-free in our heads. Forgiveness is not easy. Forgiveness does not remove the pain of the offense, but it does purify your heart from deeper issues.

When Jesus instructed us to pray, He showed the importance of forgiveness by including it in His own prayer. Jesus instructed us to pray, "Forgive us our debts, as we also have forgiven our debtors" (Matthew 6:12 NIV). This is a stark reminder that we all have a debt—an obligation we cannot pay. When we realize we have a debt we cannot pay, it helps to recognize we are flawed and imperfect and require God's forgiveness.

Jesus wanted His disciples to understand that forgiveness is a *choice*. Jesus chose to forgive our debts. The Father is waiting to forgive us. This incredible, empowering truth enables us to forgive others. When I choose to forgive, I choose to appropriate my life with Jesus.

My life was a mess and I was broken before Jesus redeemed me and called me by name. I was a debtor being held responsible for a debt I could not pay, doomed to a life of striving and shame. But God forgave me. He welcomed me as one of His own despite my offenses toward Him. It's my choice to forgive those who have hurt or offended me. Because I have been forgiven much, I freely forgive others.

We take off the emotional armor of offense when we forgive other people. We do not live in a world where offenses do not exist. We do have a choice on how we will respond when those offenses come. We also have a responsibility as believers to do everything we can to live a blameless life that does not create offense with others. We are called to be bridge builders, not bridge burners.

In Matthew 5:23–24, Jesus described how we are to approach a brother or sister who has offended us. We must keep a pure heart and operate from a place of grace in these situations of offense. God's redemption for someone else should always point us to a place of forgiveness and reconciliation. As we have been reconciled to God through Christ, we should strive to forgive those who have offended us. We imitate God when we show others mercy, grace, and forgiveness.

Rejection

There is not a person on this planet who has not experienced rejection, including Jesus. Rejection is real, and we must deal with it. First, let me explain the root of rejection.

Rejection is a form of anti-Christ on the earth. Paul tells us that Christ had one primary agenda, which was to reconcile us back to Him. He accomplished this at the cross. Second Corinthians 5:19 says, "God was reconciling the world to Himself in Christ, not counting men's trespasses against them. And He has committed to us the message of reconciliation" (BSB). God's end goal was restored relationship.

The Father sent the Son to earth with the singular mission to restore broken relationship between Him and mankind. Any person, thing, or idea that widens the gap between God and man, or between people, is an anti-Christ spirit. This spirit is against the purposes of God.

Rejection wholly opposes the very nature of God. It is a tool the enemy uses to deepen wounds, widen breaches, and separate people from one another. Rejection is a thief and works to rob and steal any asset available to it.

In John 10:10, Jesus talked about a "thief who comes only to steal and kill and destroy" (NIV). He made reference to both a thief and a robber ("steal"). I think this is paramount—that He was intentional in using each of these two specific descriptions. Jesus was emphasizing that the enemy of our soul comes as *both* a thief and a robber. A thief is "one that steals especially stealthily or secretly,"[14] while a robber takes something by force, using violence or threats.[15] Whatever seems valuable and up for the taking the enemy will scheme to take. He will use outright violent and destructive methods as well as try to manipulate in secret places to take from believers. The end goal of everything he does is to kill, steal, and destroy.

Oftentimes, the enemy will try to twist circumstances and situations so that we become disillusioned and focus on the wrong perspective, always trying to direct our attention to the wrong ideas. He sets traps for us to try to destroy our mindsets about God, life, and our identity.

Unhealed emotions of rejection can often leave an opening for the enemy to rob us.

The Latin word *reicere*, the root of the English word *reject*, means "to throw back."[16] This is an amazingly accurate description. Rejection certainly does act as a throwback to our dreams, our potential, and our future.

When rejection takes root in us, we often respond with protective behaviors first. We put up walls, and we isolate. We become hard and cynical. For fear of not being liked, we either dominate the room we are in or we just won't enter the room at all. We sometimes talk too much in order to avoid dealing with direct questions. We may become dogmatic and forceful with our own opinions and ideas. Some people respond differently and shut down completely. They will not allow their thoughts or emotions to be known.

Rejection makes us question everything important in the scheme of life. Who we are? Why are we here? Who can we trust? Rejection will cause you to turn into someone you are not; it will cause you to stifle your own identity in order to protect yourself from future rejection.

However, there is some good news! Just because you have *experienced* rejection does not mean that you have to live a life of rejection. Joseph and Mary were a great example of this principle.

Luke 2 recounts the famous story of Jesus' birth. Even though Joseph and Mary were in dire need, there was just "no room for them in the inn" (Luke 2:7 NKJV). No one was willing to give up a room for the very pregnant Mary to rest. In most cultures, anyone presented with a pregnant woman who had traveled such a long distance and was near birth would try their best to accommodate a woman in her condition. Clearly, for whatever reason, this was not the case. Ultimately, Mary and Joseph brought Jesus, the Son of God, into the arena of our natural world with animals in the cheering section. Not only did Mary and Joseph feel the realities of this rejection, but Jesus experienced it as well. He was born in a stable, among animals instead of people.

The goal of the enemy is to keep us constantly thinking we are on the outside looking in. It is his ultimate goal to keep us from experiencing belonging. It should be no surprise that Mary, Joseph, and baby Jesus all experienced the absence of belonging in this pivotal moment in history.

It is easy to read this story in the Bible and gloss over the fact that the people involved experienced real, gut-wrenching emotions. It would have been easy for Mary and Joseph to take offense and put up emotional armor toward others from that point forward. I know so many people who, when they feel rejected, become like hermits. They may not physically isolate from everyone, but they determine that they will only socialize with their friends, their family, and the few whom they have known "forever." Any new relationships are off the table because it will require vulnerability and the opportunity to be rejected once again.

The emotional armor forged by rejection does not seek retribution, but rather wants to escape all together. Escapism becomes theology. We stop spending time with people and definitely do not push ourselves out of our comfort zone, because the goal now becomes self-preservation and escape from other people's opinions.

When we want to take off emotional armor, we have to recognize that it will require vulnerability. We cannot grow without vulnerability. We must get past the comfortable and wrestle in the unknown again. We do not wrestle aimlessly but with purpose and meaning.

In *Dare to Lead,* Brene Brown says, "Choosing our own comfort over hard conversations is the very epitome of privilege."[17] It is always easier to keep the armor on and the antenna of pain up, but it is also the weakest position to live from. You exercise unrighteous privilege, almost taking advantage of the grace of God, by living with the armor you have created from rejection around you.

> And God is able to make all grace abound to you, that you, always having all sufficiency in all things, may have an abundance for every good work.
> —*2 Corinthians 9:8 NKJV*

Grace abounds toward us to do hard things. There is no lack of grace, so we can do every good work. It is a good work to let down your guard and meet a new friend. It is a good work to stop isolating and become friendly again. There is grace to let down your guard.

As a believer, we must not live beneath the benefits we have, and that means taking off this emotional armor. God is big enough to handle your pain and hurt from rejection. We must remember that we are accepted among the beloved (Ephesians 1:6). When venturing into a vulnerable place in any relationship, we must lean into the acceptance of Christ. Knowing that He has accepted us allows us to operate with an open, vulnerable heart. Our heart is always safe in the Master's hands.

Growing past rejected places means we have to replace the *rejected* place with a *received* place. Jesus told His disciples in John 14:2, "I go to prepare a place for you" (ESV). Jesus was not just giving them a glimpse of the glory land of heaven; He was also letting us know there is a place with our name on it.

When you feel rejected, bruised, and emotionally strained, remember you are accepted and loved, and there is a place God has designed just for you and you alone. Jesus came to earth in the polar opposite situation, with no place and no room in the inn, only to leave us the promise and assurance that there is always room in His inn for us. He became our place. There is a table place with your name on it, and a room set apart for you.

Do not let the troubles of this world keep you withered and dried up. When you grow over the horizons of your rejection, you find that there is seat at the prepared table just for you. Replace the rejection with your received place in Him.

Weariness

Weariness is real, especially when it is attached to unfulfilled expectations. I have found that when facing a trial, one of the most prominent demands on your life is stewardship of your *energy*.

Hardships and trials obviously wear on a person physically, but the toll on your psyche and mental energy is critical. In reality, oftentimes, your mental energy dictates your physical energy. Many people who deal with anxiety, depression, or a constant sense of condemnation are plagued with physiological issues surrounding their energy. The two are interrelated. Just as an instrument has the ability to make sound but cannot create music without a musician, our bodies need to be in tune emotionally and mentally so we can physically actualize our potential.

In 1 Kings 19, we find a familiar set of characters—Jezebel, Elijah and Ahab. Jezebel had unleashed hell on the prophets of God and swore to cause the same fate to come upon Elijah. Fearful for his life and full of weariness, Elijah escaped from Jezebel and hid out in a cave, feeling as if all of his options for a future were extinguished.

Here was one of the greatest prophets of the Old Testament, and he was contemplating dying because the circumstances around him just felt too great. He was weary. He was tired of the same battles and the same problems. He was tired of Jezebel's seemingly victorious position over the people of God, time after time. Weariness will always bring a sense of defeat and cause us to lose all sense of courage. Elijah was a great prophet who had done great and mighty things for God, but he was worn down from the battles he faced and simply forgot who he was. His courage was dissipated.

Some of the most trying seasons of my life came down to this: the struggle to remain in courage when everyone and everything happening around me only pointed to giving up and giving in to defeat. That is when courage steps in.

Courage is the ability to act *without* one hundred percent assurance. It is the ability to say yes when others are giving every reason to say no. For Elijah, at this point in his life, courage came to him when the voice from heaven reminded him of why he was on this planet. Weariness creates short-sightedness in our minds. We can only see the few inches ahead of us, and that can seem insurmountable. God comes to give us strength when we feel we cannot go on, but He cannot *make* us courageous. Courage is a response from the position of knowing and receiving God's strength.

Isaiah 40:31 says, "They who wait for the LORD shall renew their strength" (ESV). God renews strength in us, but we have to be willing to wait with a heart of faith. Weariness would like to convince you that waiting is losing, but in the Kingdom, waiting is renewing.

In Elijah's situation, he ran away from his troubles, but when he finally slowed down and got to a quiet place, God spoke. God pulled Elijah out of the hiding place he had run to in weariness. God renewed his strength by speaking purpose into him when he was in a desolate cave and thought he was all alone. Elijah felt as if he were the last prophet of God, the last man standing, but God reminded him that there were many people in the same battle, many others who were waiting on the Lord. Elijah truly was not alone.

Weariness does not only come to steal courage; it also comes to isolate us in our pain or trial. Elijah not only ran away to escape his difficult situation, but he also ran away to hide by himself. He even left his servants behind.

Isolation is a massive warning sign. Isolation is not God's desire for us. The book of Psalms says that God "sets the solitary in families" (Psalm 68:6 NKJV). He never wants us to live without a network of people in our lives. These people may not be flesh and blood, but they are like family to us.

In my experience, anytime I have isolated myself in my pain or my defeat, I have always experienced a setback in my growth. Isolation leaves us exposed to our own ways and our own thoughts, which are often misguided. Remember this quote by Allan Lokos: "Don't believe everything you think."[18] Just thinking something does not make it true. But without partnership, family, and godly relationships in your life, there is no accountability, no one to magnify the truth and dispel the lies that we often tell ourselves in solitude.

God had to remind Elijah in 1 Kings 19 that just because he *felt* alone in his mission did not mean he was actually alone in his mission. Isolation can make your situation feel hopeless. We need others to shine the light of hope in our dark places, when we cannot find the light for ourselves.

Isolation is different from insulation. Insulation, like the material used for homes and buildings, is made to help conserve and regulate energy. It is used to regulate temperature and air quality. It also helps absorb unwanted sound pollution. In this way, insulation is a huge benefit to our natural homes. In the same manner, spiritual insulation is a benefit to our spiritual homes, our spiritual lives.

However, insulation was not invented to keep people out of your home. Insulation is never described as a product or method used to keep people out of the home. The purpose of insulation is to help steward and regulate energy.

Let's look at it from a spiritual perspective. We need to put in place boundaries, warning signs, and cushioning to help us combat the energy-depleting forces that come to rob from us. And we need this thick wall to help us keep noise pollution low. However, spiritual insulation is not meant to keep people out. It is meant to protect what is from God inside our hearts, but never to keep others from accessing our heart. We simply cannot afford to put up walls of isolation in our lives.

If you have proper insulation in your life, it will ultimately be easier to build lasting, authentic relationships with others. When you have fortitude and proper building blocks in your inner life, you have the ability to do difficult things. You can easily let any "white negative noise" roll off of you because you are insulated in your soul. That kind of negative noise is deflected because you know who you are.

Insulation is a hidden help. It is a help to us when we need it, and oftentimes, you do not even realize it is working until you see the results. Learn to insulate your life with the Word of God, your prayer life, boundary strategies, and adaptability. Don't confuse insulation with the damaging forces of isolation.

Another way to insulate your life and prevent isolation is to manage your relationships well. This is a great way to steward your mental energy. When you become weary in life, the toll it takes on you mentally and physically can create a desire to pull away from others and isolate yourself like a hermit. Sometimes circumstances can become so overwhelming that we feel we just cannot handle it. Every one of us has our own unique amount of physical and mental energy. As we lean on God to renew our strength, we have to realize that we are not half-full or half-empty as much as recognize that we are refillable. God is never short on supply, and we can always come to Him to be refilled with His love and strength.

Everyone encounters weariness at some point in their journey. Everyone faces physical and mental exhaustion. How you handle weariness is the real question to be answered. Do you run and hide, or have you learned the key to sustainment?

I've learned for my own life that the key to being sustained is not a lovely two-week vacation, although breaks and time away are absolutely necessary. The practice that sustains me in the tough times is my ability to recenter. I will pull away from all the distractions in my life—turning off my phone and putting away my tablet—to sit quietly in the presence of God. I put my attention solely on Him and His goodness to center myself on the truth of who He is, in light of everything I am facing or working through. I must recenter in awareness of the season I am living in. I must recenter by prayer and meditation.

For me, meditation is a major component of how to combat weariness. Psalm 49:3 says, "My mouth shall speak wisdom, and the mediation of my heart shall give understanding" (NKJV). I often find understanding in the midst of my meditation. To discover understanding is to be able to refocus, reorient, and appropriate what is going on around you and in you. In meditation, we can evaluate our responses in order to better understand why we respond as we do.

Weariness is defeated when a heart centered on understanding prevails. When we seek to understand, we begin to wait on the Lord for His guidance, not on our own emotional promptings. *Tolerating* pain does not have reward. *Overcoming* in the midst of pain carries reward. Tolerance is not a revealer of your endurance. It actually reveals your weariness, because you wear down over time. Do not just tolerate what God says you can overcome. Everything you need to overcome is resident in you or available to you. Nothing is being withheld from you. Press into who God says you are and submit to the workings of the Holy Spirit in your life. Draw life and strength from His presence. Don't allow weariness to slow you down—you are well able to grow over it!

WORKBOOK

Chapter Three Questions

Do I trust God in this? What emotional armor are you still wearing? Offense, rejection, weariness? What is keeping you from removing it? Why are you not trusting God in these areas?

_____
_____
_____
_____
_____
_____
_____
_____
_____
_____

Who does God say I am? What does God have for you in place of offense, rejection, and weariness? How does He want you to handle or respond to each area of emotional armor? What does He speak over you?

_____

_____

_____

_____

_____

_____

_____

_____

Who do I say I am? Speak over any areas of emotional armor you are still wearing. Declare God's truth over each area. What steps do you need to take to remove emotional armor and replace it with God's hope for your life?

_____

_____

_____

_____

Chapter Three Notes

CHAPTER FOUR

A Lifestyle of Prayer

I am often asked questions about prayer like, "How do I pray?" and, "What do I say?" or I hear things like, "I don't know how to talk to God."

I totally get these sentiments. I am thankful people are not holding back their true questions about prayer and are willing to ask for help. The idea of a prayer life has often come solely from a historical perspective rather than a relational one. Add to that a misunderstanding of what prayer means biblically and it is easy to see why prayer can be a difficult topic for some to grasp.

It is imperative to have a lifestyle of prayer to grow over your situation or circumstance. I am a pastor's kid, born and bred, but I have not always understood how to pray. I grew up watching my folks pray, elders pray, and even pre-Christians pray, but it was not until I was in my early twenties that I dedicated myself to developing a prayer life.

During this time, I was participating in a distance learning program in Oklahoma City at a Christian university. When I was in town for classes, I would always stay with an incredible couple, Garnet and Frances Pike. These two heavily shaped my understanding and lifestyle of prayer.

Every day, we would end our day walking the mall indoors and praying. This was their routine, and as a young married visitor, this was also my routine while I was staying with them. During those walks, they would pray about everything. They would pray in the Spirit and pray with understanding. At first, I felt self-conscious walking and praying around a public space, but their encouragement to sense the atmosphere and devote myself to developing a prayer life was priceless.

The power of prayer has always been part of my life. I can remember hearing my granddad tell his incredible testimony. His face was completely burned in a terrible accident when a motor malfunctioned. The church elders came to the hospital and prayed for him. A few days later, the nurses removed the bandages from his face, and it was completely restored, as smooth as a baby's skin. I remember hearing my mom praying for my sisters and I during our troubling teenage years. I can remember the first time I led someone in the sinner's prayer in Siberia, Russia.

Those early experiences made a lasting impression on me. I am forever marked by observing others who are deeply devoted to God sharing with someone who never knew the hope of Jesus. Nothing compares to the joy of seeing someone come alive when they find out their life could be totally different. My heart still feels an overwhelming gratitude for the power of prayer.

Praying is not just getting on your knees and repeating words. It is so much more! Prayer is communication. Prayer is about time. Prayer is about intimacy. Prayer is about awakening. Prayer is about changing realities. Prayer is about our deepest connection. Prayer is about becoming more like Christ. It is the closest union I can feel with God. In this chapter, I want to approach a couple key areas of prayer and do my best to share what it means to have a vibrant, growing prayer life.

Why Prayer?

We have heard many times that prayer changes things. Often what changes in prayer, however, is not the emphasis on the things prayed for, but the "me" in the midst of the things. Prayer changes me. Anytime I openly bring myself to intimacy with God, I am encountering change. So, why do we pray?

First, we pray because Jesus demonstrated prayer for us. He showed us that prayer is a form of communication between God and man. It is also a door to experience and understand heaven's agenda on the earth. It is one of the key components of being in relationship with God.

Jesus demonstrated this by often leaving His disciples and finding a quiet place to pray. He tells His disciples in Matthew 6:9, "In this manner, therefore, pray" (NKJV). Jesus even instructed His disciples on how to pray.

Isn't it interesting that the disciples asked, "How should we pray?" They were observant enough to know this was part of Jesus's lifestyle. Prayer was part of His daily life, and they wanted to know how to do it, too.

When we pray, we are learning how to abide in Christ. In John 15:7, it says, "If you abide in Me, and My words abide in you, you will ask what you desire, and it shall be done for you" (NKJV). Abiding, as discussed in previous chapters, is not about carrying around a Bible, gaining more knowledge about God, or even just going to church. Abiding is about finding deep connection with God.

Leonard Sweet points out in his book, *What Matters Most*, that "belief can exist in isolation, but faith requires a relationship."[19] Prayer gives us the deep union of true relationship. Isn't that what abiding in His vine is all about—connection and union with God so that His ways become part of the engrafted ways I think and do life? Did you know we are most like ourselves when we are in prayer? Prayer changes us. Prayer changes how we pray, what we pray for, and what we pray about. If prayer is the deepest union we can experience on earth with God, then we must explore it as a gateway to gain a better understanding of God and His ways in us.

Secondly, prayer postures us. Prayer puts us in the posture of humility. Second Chronicles 7:14 tells us that when God's people humble themselves and pray, God demonstrates His power among them. He heals and delivers.

In this verse, we find two important commands. One is that we pray, but the other is the posture of that prayer: "If my people, who are called by my name, humble themselves and pray" (NIV). In other words, prayer is essential, but the posture of humility in your prayer is just as critical. Elisabeth Eliot said, "One does not surrender a life in an instant. That which is lifelong can only be surrendered in a lifetime."[20] Humility, though not a fruit of the Spirit, is very much the root of the Spirit. It is the posture of a relationship with God.

We pray so that we may enter into a posture of change and surrender. Prayer helps us to surrender repeatedly when we continue it steadfastly, as Romans 12:12 tells us. Through this surrender, we begin to see how to pray more effectively.

The "prayer of a righteous person avails much" (James 5:16 NKJV). The key, or the stipulation, for prayer is a *righteous* person praying. If your mind is consumed with what wrong has been done to you or getting even with a co-worker, then your prayer is not in righteousness. The attitude of your heart matters in what you seek from God when you pray.

Jesus said, "Seek first the kingdom of God and his righteousness, and all these things will be added to you" (Matthew 6:33 ESV). Jesus knew we could easily become people who use our prayer life to seek things that make us feel better, not necessarily praying toward the answers God has in mind. Jesus said if you learn to seek what His kingdom is doing, then you will see that He is at work, and all the other things will come as you posture yourself in Him.

Our prayer life is drawn from the "well" within our spirit. That well can be pure or contaminated, depending on what we allow to enter and cultivate in our hearts. Jesus explained this concept to the Samaritan woman in John 4:14 when He spoke of drawing from His well: "Those who drink the water I give will never be thirsty again" (NLT).

There is a well that causes you to experience natural desires differently. You can subdue even natural inclinations when you draw from the right well. This means you can pray God's will, not just your will.

When we get humble about our own understanding and start to allow the Spirit to work in us through our prayer, we begin to pray as God leads us and not just leaning into our own thoughts and earthly wisdom. Romans 8:26 reminds us that "the Spirit also helps in our weaknesses. For we do not know what we should pray for as we ought, but the Spirit Himself makes intercession for us" (NKJV). When we surrender in our prayer life, we enable our prayer time to become productive for the kingdom of God, even in ways we do not comprehend. The Holy Spirit intercedes for us and through us.

Thirdly, we pray because it sets our life on the course of consistency. One year, I was flying to Israel and there were many rabbis on board our flight. When the hours came for morning, midday, and evening prayer, if the flight was cooperative, they each got up and began their service in prayer. I have been in Africa when the horn sounds with the Muslim call to prayer seven times a day, and everyone stops and prays.

Now, some may argue that this is ritualistic, merely rote, passionless actions, but these prayers are the consistent fabric of their life. How many Christians do you know who would stop everything they are doing each day to pray? I am not denying the differences between the varying belief systems here, but I am challenging us as believers not to excuse ourselves from learning from the consistencies of those who do not believe as we do. I do not have to agree theologically with the reasoning behind the prayer rituals to value and glean from their faithfulness and consistency.

Knowing the better covenant we can experience as believers in Christ, how much more should a consistent prayer life be evident and vital! Colossians 4:2 says, "Continue earnestly in prayer, being vigilant in it with thanksgiving" (NJKV). As Christ-followers, one of the greatest characteristics we should exhibit is a consistent life. Prayer helps us to keep the consistency in our communion with God. Prayer helps us to live consistently. I have found that when I am consistent in my prayer life, everything else in my life settles into the place as it should and begins to become consistent as well.

What Prayer Is Not

Unfortunately, in our culture, prayer has been given the same status as wishful thinking and calling things into existence that are not in God's heart. Some people call it "manifestation"—putting your own hopes and dreams out in the universe, outside of any biblical basis or leading of the Spirit.

There is a story in the Bible about Jesus sending His disciples out to minister to the surrounding communities. This was their first sent assignment. He instructed them on what they were to do, how to act, and what to expect. Upon their return in Luke 10, they shared joyfully with Jesus all they saw, did, and experienced. They told Jesus about casting out demons, the healings that took place, and the unclean spirits that submitted to His name. They were rejoicing and excited about what had taken place on their first "mission."

Jesus had a different reaction. He responded by saying in Luke 10:20, "The great triumph is not in your authority over evil, but in God's authority over you" (MSG).

I have learned over the years, especially through ministering around the world, that it is easier to pray as the victim reaching for something needed than it is to stand in a place of victory. In the case of the disciples, they were most excited about how the enemy had submitted to them, but Jesus wanted them to be more excited about their own submission to Him and the Father.

Prayer is not a wishful chant or loud announcement. Jesus taught the disciples to pray in the secret place so that it was not done for show and the benefit of other's praise and admiration (Matthew 6:5–6). He was speaking of the Pharisees who openly prayed elaborate prayers that seemed eloquent but availed nothing in the Spirit because they were birthed out of the wrong motivations.

We must be careful not to allow our prayer lives to become a show or spectacle. Our lifestyle of prayer is less about what we become emboldened by and all about who we are submitting our life to. If your prayer life is just a way to garnish courage, then you are misusing it. Do you become courageous when you pray? Absolutely! But I do not pray to become courageous. I pray to become like God.

Hearing the Voice of God

How does God speak? Years ago, I was sitting in a meeting when a woman stood up and said, "When God speaks, He often sounds like you." That was an epiphany for me.

God was not going to speak to me in some booming, *Lion King* Mufasa kind of way. He was going to talk to me *like me*. The difference is that His tone is like me, but His words are not me.

God speaks to us in the language we understand. When God talks to us, it is not His intention to seem distant or unapproachable. It is quite the opposite! God wants our communication to come from the root of our relationship. It is no wonder He chooses to sound like us, yet not be us at all. He wants us to know He is in us, working on our behalf.

Sometimes His words are few. Sometimes they are pricks in our heart. Sometimes His words are small leanings in a certain direction. Sometimes His words are audible. God never withholds from us. He is always speaking. If you are having trouble hearing His voice, try to slow down and simply listen. Learn to wait on Him.

Part of Paul's instruction to the Thessalonians was to "pray without ceasing" (1 Thessalonians 5:17 NKJV). Clearly, to stay in your prayer closet all day is impossible. So, how do we pray without ceasing? By keeping ourselves attentive to God and His voice in us. Tune your ears so that you are leaning into His voice throughout your day.

When prayer is a lifestyle, you do not need a set time to pray that is the only time you hear from God or He hears from you. A consistent, daily quiet time of prayer is key, but we have the ability and privilege to live in a constant sense of union with God in the midst of our everyday lives.

When I live with the consciousness that God is with me (Emmanuel), I live open to hearing Him often and throughout my day. The problem lies in our unwillingness to let God into our compartmentalized lives. We can so easily compartmentalize God and our faith to the point that we literally cut off communication with Him during our day. We get caught up with the "I got this" kind of attitude or, "This is my area, God," kind of ways.

We often shut God out unintentionally. As a result, we do not leave any space for Him to speak to us. The Psalmist wrote that we must incline our ear to hear (Psalm 17:6 NKJV). We must intentionally allow our hearts to be open to hear what God wants to say. He is waiting to speak; we only need a listening ear and receptive heart.

Praying in the Spirit

Your prayer life goes to a different place when you learn how to pray in the Spirit. First Corinthians 14:2–4 essentially teaches that our prayer language is communication belonging to you and God. When we pray in the Spirit by praying in tongues, we are communicating mysteries to ourselves.

Praying in the Spirit edifies us—according to Jude 1:20 (MSG) and 1 Corinthians 14:4—and enables us to pray beyond our own surface understanding. Think of your prayer language this way. To run programs that we all recognize and utilize on our computers, we have codes embedded into our electronic devices. These codes, though only understood by code readers, release permission and give commands to our devices so that they will do what they are expected to do. When this works properly, our programs perform with integrity and at the level of expectation.

Similarly, God codes our lives with the code of heaven. This is often released to us through praying in the Spirit. It is God coding our "devices" and speaking a different language to the programs that are operable in our lives. Some argue that speaking in tongues is no longer existent. However, praying in tongues is one of the forms of expressing that God has filled our hearts and lives.

He does not fill us to make us better than anyone else but so that we can reveal His fullness to others. Praying in the Spirit is crucial to take your prayer life to a deeper place in God. When I do not know how to run the programs of my life, I seek the Coder for the answers. I do not need to understand it all, but I do need to know that God is able to work through my life as I pray in the Spirit.

WORKBOOK

Chapter Four Questions

Do I trust God in this? Take time to evaluate your current prayer life. In what ways can you deepen your prayer life and connection with God?

_____
_____
_____
_____
_____
_____
_____
_____
_____
_____

Who does God say I am? How do you see yourself in your approach to God in prayer? What is your posture? What role does the Holy Spirit play in your prayer time?

_____

_____

_____

_____

_____

_____

_____

_____

_____

_____

Who do I say I am? Think about a time when you clearly heard the voice of God for yourself. What is the Holy Spirit saying to you today?

_____

_____

_____

_____

_____

_____

Chapter Four Notes

CHAPTER FIVE

The Armor of God

When I was starting out as a young leader, I was given the opportunity to teach a course on the whole armor of God. It was a course designed to help grow our young people in a better understanding of what it means to really be on the defense spiritually. This teaching assignment was part of a college course on prayer at that time. When I first received this assignment, I was a bit confused. I thought to myself, "Why would I ever have to be on the defense in God, and how do I actually do that in prayer?" It made absolutely no sense to me.

My husband and I love football. One day, I heard someone discussing the outcome of a game and they said this common phrase in the football world: "Defense wins championships." As so many analysts and recliner quarterbacks have concluded, football championships are not won by the offense but by the defense. Teams are only as great as their defense.

Something clicked with this commentary. There is a difference between being defended and being defensive. This was why we can utilize a defensive posture in prayer! In Ephesians 6:11, Paul instructed the people of Ephesus to "put on the whole armor of God" (NKJV). This armor is a completely different view on armor than discussed in our previous chapter. The pieces of this armor that are mentioned in Ephesians 6 are all protective, except for one special piece of equipment. Paul was writing to Christ-followers, or people of the Way, who were living in a hostile environment. These early Christians were facing a tremendously contrary culture that kept them in the minority of every political, public, and educational arena.

Paul was well-aware of the position of the church in Ephesus in this culture. They were underdogs who could easily be attacked and overtaken. They were susceptible to being taken advantage of and singled out for persecution. However, Paul did not want the early Christians to see their position as weak or as in need of physical protection. They were part of a different Kingdom. Paul encouraged these believers to see that God had laid out spiritual articles ready to help them walk out a life in a difficult place so they could be defended without becoming defensive.

When Paul wrote to the Ephesians "to put on the whole armor of God," he meant to clothe oneself. This had the same meaning as when we tell our kids to go put on their clothes for school or for bedtime. Paul was showing that one of the primary ways you will find the tenacity and the fortitude you need to overcome the hostile world you have been called to is to learn to put on the clothes that have been already laid out for you in God.

Peace, righteousness, truth, and faith are all weapons and armor in the arsenal of God, given to man. These are not just attributes; they are the very image of God Himself stamped out in us. We cannot interpret and apply this passage to our lives as those seeking a fight but only as those who are equipped with the right safety gear to encounter any unknown enemy. Like the padding that protects the knees, elbows, and chin when a child is riding a bike, so this armor of God protects us spiritually. We can navigate spiritual battles with the confidence that we are safe and our vulnerable areas are covered by the very armor God has provided for us.

The Belt of Truth

As we continue adding the pieces of this armor, Paul tells us to "[put] on the belt of truth" (NLT). The truth is the "belt" in our lives that holds it all together. It holds up our spiritual pants so we do not show our backside!

Truth is not a thing or an object. Truth is a Person: Jesus is the Truth. He is our connecting point, holding us together. We must hold onto His truth and not lean into our own ideas and strategies. Paul was instructing us to tie ourselves up with what cannot be untied, which is the truth of God.

Just to go on record, the truth is truth whether you believe it or not! Truth applied to your life is power in motion. When we realize that Jesus is living truth, we set our lives to learn of Him. Girding ourselves with truth is not merely speaking the Bible over your circumstances but, more so, learning to live out a relationship with Jesus Himself as Truth. He is our plumbline.

The Breastplate of Righteousness

The next part of the armor that Paul describes is the breastplate of righteousness. The book of Jeremiah says, "The heart is deceitful above all things" (Jeremiah 17:9 ESV). When you are in desperate situations, it is easy for your heart to become defeated and downcast. It is easy to let anxiety rob you of perspective.

Instead of letting your heart take the lead, guard your heart with the breastplate of righteousness. Righteousness means to be made right and for your accounts to be balanced with God. We can have the right thinking no matter the situation. When we protect our lives with His righteousness, we resist following our own thoughts and desires.

God's kingdom seldom plays by the rules of this world. I cannot tell you how many times I have experienced someone being correct but still very wrong. They were right on the issue but wrong in how they dealt with their "rightness." We cannot afford to value being right above staying in sync with God's righteousness. Someone else has made us righteous, and He is the only worthy One among us. Putting on the breastplate of righteousness is an act of faith, knowing that the righteousness of God will protect our heart. It means laying down our will and allowing God to be our defense.

When Jesus was arrested and brought to trial, the chief priests and all His accusers were like dogs at a fight yearning for Him to get in the arena with them. But we see His response to their attacks and accusations in Luke 23:9: "[Jesus] answered him nothing" (NKJV). He showed us that it is possible to be mocked, ridiculed, maligned, and lied about, yet still walk out of the courtroom without having to make a case for ourselves.

Defensiveness is always an indication of a misunderstanding for what God has already done for us. When we carry His righteousness over our heart, we do not have to defend ourselves. We are fully aware that we were unworthy and He saw fit to make room for us regardless of our unworthiness. Titus 3:5 says, "He saved us, not because of righteous things we had done, but because of His mercy" (NIV). We have the freedom to rest in the knowledge of our security in Him. He is our righteousness and our defense.

Feet Shod with Peace

After the breastplate of righteousness, Paul described an interesting part of this protective armor of God. He said to "shod your feet with the preparation of the gospel of peace" (Ephesians 6:15 NKJV).

What does it mean to "shod your feet?" I believe this means to stay alert and ready. It is imperative today to be a person of prepared peace, alert to the schemes of the enemy. When Paul was writing to the church in Ephesus, he was encouraging the believers to stay ready and alert to share the good news of peace in all ways.

Every place we go, everywhere our feet touch, and everything we say and do should drip with the honeycomb of peace. One of our greatest defenses against the tactics of the enemy is to remain in peace and bring peace whenever we go.

Jesus taught in Matthew 5:9, "Blessed are the peacemakers, for they shall be called the sons of God" (NKJV). One of the ways to recognize a son or daughter of God is by the peace surrounding their life. Peace is a part of the character of God. Jesus did not come to bring judgments but to restore peace. Peace is a strategy! The gospel message is a message of peace. It is God's desire that we calm storms through His peace.

In Hebrew, the word *shalom* has many meanings, including "peace" and "wholeness."[21] Wherever there is *shalom*, there is wholeness. When we encounter breaches in ourselves, others, or circumstances, we must allow the shalom of God to come and build us back up. We allow His peace to heal, restore, and bind up these breaches with His wholeness.

The Shield of Faith

Ephesians 6:16 reads, "Above all, taking the shield of faith with which you will be able to quench all the fiery darts of the wicked one" (NKJV). Let me tell you what faith is not. It is not wishful thinking or denying present circumstances. It is not denial or empty, unproductive religious talk.

Faith is earnest expectation. It is the ability to keep believing and initiate believing when things are contrary.

Jesus said effective prayer is not found in the loud or boastful (Matthew 6:5–9), but it is born from a seed of faith. Jesus said, "If you have faith as a mustard seed, you will say to this mountain, 'Move from here to there,' and it will move" (Matthew 17:20 NKJV).

This was not just an analogy about the size of our faith but also about the form of our faith. The comparison of the size of the mustard seed to our faith is usually highlighted in this passage. It is a great example of a tiny seed in contrast to the grandeur of a full-grown tree. Yet I also think it speaks to the form of our faith by describing a seed. What do you do with a seed? You plant it. You invest it. You sow it for future harvest.

Faith is not only able to start small, but it is also able to grow big. Faith is a seed. You plant that seed of faith when it is dark and dirty. You plant the seed when it is rainy and wet. Your seed grows best in places many people refuse to go. This is also true in dealing with the shield of faith. Paul said it will work as a guard against the darts of the enemy. When planted properly, the seed of faith can disband the darts of the enemy. In difficult situations, continue to plant those seeds of faith around you. Do not shut down and withdraw inward with your thoughts and anxieties. Be a planter of faith and draw up the shield of faith around you.

The Helmet of Salvation

Another piece of armor that we must wear in any spiritual battle is the helmet of salvation. Your mind is the battlefield of your soul. When Paul reminded the

Ephesians to defend themselves by wearing the helmet of salvation, he was reminding them to remember salvation is always at hand. When your mind wants to retreat or entertain thoughts that do not represent the mind of Christ, remember to "put on the mind of Christ" and draw from the wells of salvation as a redeemed child of God.

Renewing your mind is about reestablishing truth as the highest function of forming you as a person. My father likes to say it this way: "Whatever is informing you is forming you." Our thoughts shape our being. We must be diligent to renew our minds and assess what we are allowing to inform us and form us. Renewing your mind means washing it with the Word and doing away with any thoughts or ideas that do not align with God's Word and God's ways.

We also put on the helmet of salvation so that our mind does not deceive us. The Psalmist wrote "Restore to me the joy of your salvation" (Psalm 51:12 NIV). There is a joy that comes with our salvation. There is an awareness of what God has done for us through Jesus. When we keep this in the center of our minds, we can step into our lives differently.

In Matthew 6, when Jesus was instructing the disciples on how to pray, He instructed us to pray and live in the same way we are forgiven so that we, too, will forgive. The instruction was to first remember what God has done for you. Recall just how broken and inept you were and then, from that place, find the courage and wisdom to bring forgiveness to others.

I am deeply convinced most people struggle to forgive or find joy in the journey, and are full of anxiety, because they are living without this canopy of defense. They are living without the helmet of their salvation, so they cannot view the world through the eyes of God and they struggle to clearly understand His purposes and plans.

The Sword of the Spirit

The only offensive piece of the armor of God mentioned in Paul's description is a weapon—the "sword of the Spirit." This is significant to us as believers. The Spirit of God is not given to us as a defensive strategy but rather to empower us on the offense! It is our guarantee that God will do what He said He will do.

The sword of the Spirit is a skillful tool in the hands of the defender. Billy Graham said, "The sword of the Spirit—the Bible—is the weapon God has provided for us to use in this battle between truth and deception."[22] Therefore, to use the sword of the Spirit is to skillfully and accurately know how to use the Word the God. This is vital in our culture today because many do not study the Bible to understand God's Word but rather to validate their own words, thoughts, or emotions.

The Bible has been used for centuries to validate undeniable falsehoods such as slavery and discrimination against women or other segments of society. Yet, we must see that this book, the Bible, is not about discovering the justification for your own arguments but about discovering the content of God's goodness.

Graham went on to encourage us to "make it a priority to wield that Sword skillfully."[23] When we understand that the Word is a weapon for us to use in spiritual battles, we must reassess our use of Scripture and our own biblical understanding.

Several years ago, I heard a teaching by Leonard Sweet on the difference between observing an animal in its natural habitat and observing an animal piece by piece in a lab, or our human habitat. He drew a comparison that we often approach God, and therefore Scripture, with the second approach rather than the first. We put God into our habitat and try to make sense of Him one petri dish at a time rather than letting God be God and observing Him in His own habitat. The created ones try to define the Creator and His Word, in a sense.

If we merely observe God as laboratory scientists, we may make out some of His "DNA" or characteristics, but we miss the essence of how He uses them in our lives. This type of examination will ultimately lead us to misjudge and misappropriate His ways and even His Word.

When we are becoming skillful in our handling of God's Word, we will never assign to it an agenda birthed on the earth. Just like a real sword takes time to learn how to handle skillfully and properly, we must spend time seeking God to understand. If not, we can bring harm to ourselves and others by using the Word improperly.

God's Word is an eternal book and requires eternal thinking. To become skillful in the Word of God, we must look at Scripture through both the historical context and the prophetic context. We do not worship the book; we worship the Jesus of the book. John 1 tells us the Word became flesh. His name was Jesus. The sacred Scripture is not just the sixty-six books we have downloaded on a Bible app on our phones or carry in our arms bound between leather. Learning the Word is learning a Person. We are getting to know and become like Him. It is so important to learn to use His Word rightly.

Armored for a Purpose

The importance of the entire armor of God—these figurative garments that have a huge impact on our lives—is that we can truly become more effective in our prayer lives and in our mission for Christ. I often ask the Lord to help me in these areas in my life. I desire to carry the sword of the Spirit rightly and to know how to divide the word of God in my circumstances.

I pray that my faith will arise and grow so that the fiery darts of the enemy will not find a breach in my shield. I pray that I will be a peacemaker, not just a peace talker. I pray that I will carry the peace of God in all that I do, everywhere I go. I pray that I will not forget where I was brought out of, so that I can minister effectively to those who are still in the fight. I pray that truth will lead me beyond my understanding and that my commitment to be a woman of integrity may be evident in all I do. I pray that my heart will walk in alignment with my spirit man and that I will be righteous in my soul. I pray that I will not shy away from the world I have been called to, but will walk in humility so that I can do what I have been called to do. This is my prayer, and this is my commitment. May it be yours also!

WORKBOOK

Chapter Five Questions

Do I trust God in this?

_____
_____
_____
_____
_____
_____
_____
_____
_____
_____
_____
_____

Who does God say I am? Which part of the armor of God do you most easily "wear"? Which part is more difficult for you to identify?

_____
_____
_____
_____
_____
_____
_____
_____
_____

Who do I say I am? How do you renew your mind?

_____
_____
_____
_____
_____
_____
_____

Chapter Five Notes

CHAPTER SIX

Hostile Environments

Hostile environments are inevitable. A hostile environment is inhospitable; it is "not friendly, warm, or generous."[24] Hostile environments are intentionally ungenerous and consciously set against something or someone.

No one is immune to encountering a hostile environment at some point in life. No one outruns pain. No one outruns difficulty. You cannot be rich enough to stop it, nor poor enough to avoid it. Hostile environments are simply part of the bigger picture of God's growth mechanism for our lives. We can draw comfort from the fact that even those closest to Jesus, His chosen twelve disciples, experienced many adverse circumstances while walking with the Master.

Although you cannot escape hostile conditions in this life, you are not bound to live subject to them. In Matthew 14:24–25, Jesus and the disciples were in a ship in the middle of the sea, which was tossed by waves, "for the wind was contrary" (NKJV). But guess what? The next verse tells us how Jesus dealt with those contrary waves tossed by the wind—*He walked on them.*

I believe that God really desires to walk on the waves of our lives more often than we invite Him. We are so distracted by the environment or the circumstance that we lose supernatural perspective in Him and in us. This passage in Matthew reminds us that with just the right amount of out-of-the-box thinking, anything is possible! This is the famous story of Peter walking on the water, but do we see this as a one-off anomaly? Is this just a biblical story to encourage us, or is it seriously a way to pattern our lives?

Let's look at this water-walking story from two perspectives. First, let's analyze the situational circumstances for the disciples in the boat with Jesus. Then we can examine how everyone involved actually responded to this unusual environment and what that means for us as believers.

A Contrary Wind

Matthew 14:24 clearly describes the physical environment: the wind was "contrary" (NKJV), or set against the boat. This is pivotal information. Keep in mind that some of the fellows on the boat were experienced seamen and would have been somewhat accustomed to this type of windy weather from their fisherman days. Wind is "the perceptible natural movement of the air".[25] Wind is not always perceived outside of observing what the wind influences.

In this story, the wind plays a key role in the instability the disciples were feeling. An invisible force was causing experienced fisherman to sit up and take notice. We, too, experience wind around our floating ships of life. We are content that we are in the boat crossing the water, but once the wind begins to blow, panic sets in!

Often, this experience arises from invisible forces in our lives as well. The "contrary winds" could be your thought life, your circumstances, or any obstacle that you encounter unexpectedly. Your "boat" must be able to withstand these contrary winds and, by faith, stay the course.

As if the winds were not enough to stress the disciples, their boat also began to rock and sway in the middle of the sea. Now, some of us folks do not mind rocking the boat. When you have complete control of a situation, rocking the boat can honestly be fun. However, the disciples were not in control in this situation—they were in open water, with gall-force winds rocking their boat, without life jackets.

The boat that was to transport them to the next destination safely was failing them in the middle of the sea.

Sinking Confidence

These men, some experienced fishermen, were now losing confidence quickly because the integrity of their transportation was diminishing by the minute. The high winds were too much. This just reminds me of how many times we put our lives in the wrong vessels.

In this story, we all tend to highlight the obviously spectacular event of Peter walking on water to Jesus, but we forget that at the same time, Peter's counterparts had chosen to put all of their confidence in the ability of the boat, not Jesus. I realize no one knew for certain what was going on and that Jesus was actually going to walk out to them on the waves, defying natural laws. But the disciples *had* experienced life with Jesus up to this point and *did* know that He was the better vessel to depend on. Why did they not trust that Jesus was bigger than their own boat's engineering?

I believe they simply trusted more in what they were feeling and what they were seeing in the moment. Because the boat was being tossed around and beaten up in the waves and winds, all they could focus on was the destruction and danger. So often, this is the case with us as well. We put our confidence in what we are "riding in" rather than trusting in who we are riding *with*. We value the vessel itself more than the God of the vessel.

Maybe our job is the vessel we are riding in, but as soon as we hit a bump with a new boss who doesn't see eye to eye, we start questioning whether God wants us to work there. Maybe our vessel is our health and we suddenly encounter the "contrary wind" of a negative medical report. Maybe the vessel is your business or your home. These things are great, but ultimately temporal and not worthy of our trust. Only God deserves our full confidence. When our trust is placed in any other vessel, we end up living like the disciples—panicked and afraid, believing that we are going to sink at any moment.

Getting Out of the Boat

Let's fast forward now to the big moment in this story: Peter's remarkable move. Peter had no reason to get out of the boat other than the fact that he thought he could. I love that about Peter. He was smart enough to change tactics and naïve enough to do it alone and believe it would work!

No one else got out of the boat that day. Everyone else was satisfied with seeing Jesus but not necessarily joining Him on the water. This is so often the case in many believers' lives. We become satisfied that Jesus is with us but we never engage the higher call—to become *like* Him.

The Bible says God is omnipresent (see Psalm 139:7–10). He is everywhere. He is in all and through all. We do not have the ability to determine when God will show up. However, we do have the privilege to recognize and invite His presence into our every moment.

Sometimes we tend to believe that recognizing and having an awareness of God's presence is the highest point of spiritual development. In actuality, our upward call is to adhere to Jesus' words to become more like Him and make disciples. Matthew 28:18–20 (NKJV) says:

> *And Jesus came and spoke to them, saying, "All authority has been given to Me in heaven and on earth. Go therefore and make disciples of all of the nations, baptizing them in the name of the Father and of the Son and of the Holy Spirit, teaching them to observe all things that I have commanded you; and lo, I am with you always, even to the end of the age."*

Jesus explained to His disciples that we have been given this authority, not as a way to be with God or to secure our place in heaven but so we can "go and make disciples." It's a higher call.

In Peter's case, no one can know exactly what drove him to ask Jesus if he could join Him. All we know is that he asked. He clearly saw that Jesus' authority was capable of supporting his life in unexplored ways.

Exploring His Mystery

When was the last time you saw Jesus' authority and power capable of supporting you into the unknown? For Peter, he decided to change vessels, deciding not to put his confidence in what had been dependable and predictable transportation in his life experience. Instead, he put his confidence in the unexplainable yet totally visible power of God.

Real transformation to grow over the walls of opposition of our lives does not come in the safety of well-known places in God. Real transformation comes from exploring the unknown, the mystery of God. For Peter, that night all the wind, waves, and circumstances disappeared and he connected with the mystery of God. Peter's understanding of God merged with his expectant hopes and thoughts of Him. Peter longed to be like Jesus and do what Jesus had done, however, impossible-seeming, so he was prepared to take a risk. We may not ever walk on physical water, but each one of us has the opportunity to walk on terrain in our lives that appears to be impassable.

Six years ago, I experienced my own mystery with God by boarding a plane to fly to Uganda to minister at a pastor's conference with primarily male pastors. As I have shared in previous chapters, this was a moment of walking off my own map.

I became like Peter in that moment and stepped out of my boat onto unknown and unsteady terrain. Most people thought I would sink, but instead, what was meant to swallow me up actually became like concrete under my feet.

On my second trip to Uganda the following year, I was introduced to a very powerful man and his wife in a hotel lobby. They were there to meet a mutual friend, and I had come down for dinner. As I came into the dining hall, my friend stopped me and introduced me to this couple. This was at the end of my day, and I was just freshly showered but in my loungewear. I was not looking to meet with anyone and certainly never would have stopped if my friend had not insisted.

As I stood there, the man introduced his wife and himself. We had a brief, cordial conversation together. When I went to shake his hand before he left, he said these words to me: "When you really want to make a difference and get big crowds, call me. I know a lot of powerful people and for the right price can get you in any environment." It was an "aha" moment for me.

For years, I had watched my dad, an internationally known speaker and leader in the faith, navigate this world. There are always two sides of power in any nation: God's kingdom and the kingdoms of the world. We can interact with both kingdoms, but only one of them carries life. While he was still shaking my hand, I simply responded,

"Thank you, but no thanks. Either God does it, or it will not be done." I let go of his hand and walked to my table. That was the last encounter we ever had.

Today, that gathering in Uganda, which began with about one hundred and fifty pastors, has grown to an established regional conference, with more than one thousand pastors and leaders attending annually. The growth we have seen with that conference had nothing to do with worldly tactics but came from just continuing to believe in the unknown when I was not sure how it would happen. When God shows up, water often turns to concrete! This is the beautiful mystery of the power of God at work. No one can explain it other than to say we stopped being conditioned to our conditions and became explorers of His mystery at work in us.

How to Step Out of the Boat

So, how do you step out of the boat in your life? *First, when contrary winds are around you, you must learn to refuel your faith.* When difficult conditions come into your life, the first thing to be tested is your faith. In 1 Timothy 6, Paul told Timothy to "fight the good fight of faith" (verse 12 NKJV). Faith is refueled by leading ourselves back to the center—to the personhood of Christ. In my most troubling moments, I must refocus on the core elements of why I believe as I believe. I have to re-solidify why I am doing what I am doing.

This past year, I encountered some health issues unexpectedly. The doctor told me I had to make some significant adjustments in order to solve them. This was a tough pill to swallow for me. I would have to change so much of my lifestyle in order to overcome these issues. But every time I felt a hint of anxiety or distraction, I would remind myself why I am doing this. The reason gave me the endurance to carry on.

The same goes for any difficult circumstance. We must contend for our faith. In other words, you must grapple with doubt and come out stronger! You must be determined to overcome. You must refocus, recenter, and reestablish what and in Whom you believe. Faith is not built by grit but by confidence in the One who will make a way where there seems to be no way.

Secondly, we make a move to step out of the boat when we become so uncomfortable that we can no longer stay where we are inside the boat. Sometimes God will absolutely disrupt your life to move you into a new place.

Noah is a wonderful example. I believe the ark that Noah built was less about keeping him and his family safe and more about getting Noah into his next assignment. Was it a place of safety? Yes. But ultimately, the ark was the vehicle into a new day for Noah and his family. I am certain that Noah fought through some uncomfortable days. Building a vessel no one had ever heard of, preaching about an event no one had ever experienced, and living with animals he had never taken care of—of course Noah was uncomfortable! But God used Noah's obedience in the midst of his discomfort to move him into a new location, both physically and spiritually.

We have to be willing to let God make us uncomfortable. If God cannot offend you with His plans, I question your submission to Him. God has often used circumstances out of my control, not to break me down but to awaken me to new possibilities that were not visible to me because of my own routine and well-ordered plans. It is easy to disregard new things and stick with the comfort of the known.

I live in a small town. For years, we had no coffee shops and had to get our coffee from the local gas stations. Naturally, I became accustomed to leaving my small town to journey into the city when I wanted that latte, coffee-shop feel.

Recently, we had a coffee shop finally open in our little town. I and my husband, Jason, were so excited to finally have some new options, so we tried it. Was it good? Yes. Was it better than my coffee shops farther away? No. But we end up going there more often, anyway. Why? Because the convenience of the coffee shop in town has greater value to us than the quality of the coffee shop in the city. We will often tolerate mediocre coffee in our lives because it is comfortable and convenient rather than press ourselves to go a little farther for something much better. It really is worth the effort. We must get uncomfortable in order to step out of the boat.

Third, we must become more biblically literate. This is a big one for me. Our culture is largely biblically illiterate. Sure, we have quotable scriptures that make us feel good and are encouraging to post and share, but most people do not understand the contextual application of these scriptures.

We are accustomed to hearing certain stories, scriptures, and sermons to the point that they no longer carry weight for us. They become mundane and almost lifeless to us in many ways. The Bible is our guidebook. It is life-giving and truth-checking. Many Christians depend on the Sunday morning message to gain knowledge and yet never study and apply the teachings beyond that one hour a week. We are meant to learn from the Word of God so we can continually be changed into the likeness of Christ.

The principles from the Word are life-giving and offer guidance to our soul and spirit. These principles are lifestyle checks and warnings. Each character in Scripture gives us a new and deeper understanding of the nature of God and His ways, which are all so much higher than ours.

The Bible is not just my compass but also my indication for wrong thinking. Just like the "check engine" light on the dashboard of a car, the Word gives us an indication in our hearts when things are not working properly. Second Corinthians 3:18 says, "But we all, with unveiled face, beholding as in a mirror the glory of the Lord, are being transformed into the same image from glory to glory, just as by the Spirit of the Lord" (NKJV). Unlike Moses or those under the Old Covenant, we have access to God through Jesus to allow the light of the Word to reflect in our hearts and call us up to the standard of Christ. The Word of God is beautiful, full of love and grace. It reflects the heart of the Father, which is always good, gracious, and true.

There are multiple ways to study Scripture. Some people choose devotionals to help them study. Others will dive into a specific book of the Bible looking for deeper meaning and understanding to apply to their lives. Many people join accountability groups that help them establish a habit of reading and applying God's Word. There is no right or wrong way. The most important thing is that you start somewhere.

When I gave my life to God, I started reading a chapter of Proverbs every day. This was an easy start because there are thirty-one chapters in the book of Proverbs, which is considered a "wisdom book." I definitely wanted more wisdom in my life, and this was a great beginning to my study of the Word.

I also wanted to understand the character of Christ with more depth and aptitude, so I started reading the book of John in the New Testament. I love how this book presents Jesus as fully God and fully human.

I needed to know how to live this Christian life, and these books were great launching places for my walk with Christ. I realize that some folks may be way beyond this simplistic approach to the Scriptures. Let me encourage you to keep a hunger for knowledge. Do not let what you think you know keep you from what you need to know. Every time I approach Scripture as the "expert," I lose an opportunity to grow.

There is a reason Jesus tells us we must have faith like a child (see Matthew 18:3). We must be novices each and every time we come to the Bible; otherwise, we apply scriptures out of context to fit our religious thinking. Always approach the Word with an open heart and teachable spirit. God is always waiting to teach you something new!

Fourth, stepping out of the boat takes faith, but it does not have to mean going to battle over the wrong things. There are no spoils in stepping out of the boat just to show everyone you can do it. Make sure you are fighting the right fights. If the step forward is just to remind those who are behind you that you were capable, you may be fighting the wrong fight.

Paul told Timothy in 1 Timothy 6:12, "Fight the good fight of faith" (NKJV). In Greek, the word "good" that Paul used here actually means "suitable."²⁶ In other words, Paul was telling Timothy to be sure to fight only the fights suited or tailored for him.

I know so many people who are not fighting suitable fights. They are fighting, gritting their teeth, bearing down on their issues, but have never taken the time to determine if the fight is even intended for them. Fighting suitable fights is not about grit. It is about grace. What are you graced to do?

Romans 11:6 reminds us, if we obtain by works alone, then grace is no longer grace. Grace is an enablement to do what you have to do. Grace is found, and grace is given. James 4:6 says, "But He gives more grace" (NKJV). James confirmed that grace is given to us! God's empowerment and enablement to do unthinkable things is given to us. We can step out of the boat in His grace.

Grace is also found. Hebrews 4:16 says, "Let us therefore come boldly to the throne of grace, that we may obtain mercy and find grace to help in time of need" (NKJV). We can find the grace we need for the battles ahead.

It is so important to know the Word of God and the full context by the Spirt of God. In a day when anyone can post and share, we have more lies and untruths coming at us than ever before. Even well-meaning followers of Christ can unknowingly share lies and half-truths and not lead well.

For example, a preacher or teacher can say things like, "Nothing is impossible to you," and everyone will shout, like, comment, and share! However, the truth is, there are many, many things that are impossible for us, even for sold-out, on-fire Christians. It is impossible for me to walk on water without Jesus' power working in me. It is impossible for me to become my best self without the wisdom of God and the support of others. It is impossible for me to know myself without trusted confidants. It is impossible for me to just do whatever I want when God says in Psalm 16 that He has chosen boundaries for me. It tickles our ears to hear that nothing is impossible for us, but in reality, that is not the context of the Scripture at all.

Nothing is impossible for *God.* Whatever grace and enablement we need to accomplish our God-given tasks we possess only through God's power working in us. We do not have to fear insurmountable tasks. Whether it be a starting a business, navigating a family dilemma, walking out singleness after a divorce, dealing with infertility, or whatever the situation, we know that we can overcome the fight only by the power of God.

What seems impossible to us is possible through Him. These fights are suitable fights because they come with the grace needed to grow over it. Does it make them easy and painless? Probably not. However, when we can discern which fights are suitable for us, then the circumstances no longer control us. We can fight the good fight of faith by leaning into the power of God in each situation.

Finally, if you want to learn to step out of the boat and into your next, you must have understanding in light of eternity.

> *I have seen the God-given task with which the sons of men are to be occupied. He has made everything beautiful in its time. Also He has put eternity in their hearts.*
> **—Ecclesiastes 3:10–11a** NKJV

Years ago, I was reading the book of Ecclesiastes during my devotional time. I find Solomon's words inspiring and interesting, especially concerning times and seasons. I love how, even as the wisest man in Scripture at that time, Solomon was so openly vulnerable about the vanity and fruitlessness of some endeavors. I am so thankful to read about someone else who has lived out fruitless decisions, too!

Like Solomon, I have sometimes found myself like the dog in the old adage—chasing the car and finding that once it's caught, there is not much I can do with it! Fortunately, I know I am not the only one who has invested time, money, and resources into things that are temporary, hoping for eternal outcomes.

It's interesting to consider how we try to inform an eternal God about our temporal issues. In Ecclesiastes 3, Solomon helps us understand that we cannot escape the rhythms and seasons of life and the role they have on our life's journey. Solomon says that although we cannot change seasons, God has still planted eternity in our hearts in the midst of them. Wow! What a valuable insight. When I read that God has put eternity in man's heart, it helps me understand that even in the midst of difficulties, painful experiences, and unpredictable times, we can live our lives in light of the eternal value, not just the temporal view.

I am convinced that Joseph had this eternal view to endure the trouble that came his way. He had a sense of eternal value that kept him close to God even when he did not understand what was happening around him. Sometimes as Christians, we think we are going to live at a constant emotional high and that every season will be a mountaintop, only to discover that this is far from reality.

As one of my heroes in the faith, Elisabeth Elliot, put it, "The will of God is never exactly what you expect it to be. It may seem to be much worse, but in the end, it's going to be a lot better and a lot bigger."[27]

Sent by God

I love Elisabeth Elliot's story.[28] She was a mother, wife, and missionary who would not be deterred from her purpose, even when her husband Jim was murdered by the Huarorani tribe, the very people with whom they were sharing the gospel. In the midst of her pain, Elisabeth still found light in her God and in her assignment. She even returned to the Huarorani people to bring them the Good News, to carry on the assignment that her husband began.

She is a testimony of true grace and living in light of eternity. Even after tragedy, she carried on. She lived wanting life for those dead in sin more than wanting to hold them accountable for her husband's death. To live in the light of eternity does not mean to live unaware, but fully aware. You become fully aware of your motivations, your actions and your journey.

The writer of Psalm 105:17 said of Joseph that he was a "sent" man, not just a sold man. His journey was now being recorded in light of eternity. What looked like a sale for profit by his brothers meant to bring harm was actually a greater plan to send Joseph on assignment for an entire generation.

The word *sent* used here in Hebrew can also mean to sow.[29] It is the same word used in Isaiah 6:8 when the Lord Himself said to Isaiah, "Whom shall I send? And who will go for us?" (NIV).[30] When we look at this word with greater depth and apply the rich meaning, we realize that God sows us into the world to be seeds of His loins so that we can reap a great harvest for Him. Our lives are sent.

Joseph was sent. He might have experienced hardship, and he might have felt out of control at times, but ultimately God sowed him into his generation for "such a time as this" (Esther 4:14). Perhaps we could begin to see our lives in light of eternity; remember, as Ecclesiastes 3:11 says, God has "set eternity in the human heart." Our lives have eternal destiny, and God has purposed us to impact not only our generation, but also generations to come.

We are actually seeds of God sown into the earth for His purposes. When we view our world through the light of His eternity, we can place ourselves in the big picture of grace. Life takes on a new perspective. I love this quote, which has often been attributed to Mother Teresa: "I alone cannot change the world, but I can cast a stone across the waters to create many ripples." It's time to step out of the boat and make some waves.

WORKBOOK

Chapter Six Questions

Do I trust God in this? In what areas has God called you to step out of your "boat"? What fears or thoughts may be holding you back? What are some ways that you fortify your faith and trust to say "yes" to God's call?

_____
_____
_____
_____
_____
_____
_____
_____

Who does God say I am?

Who do I say I am?

Chapter Six Notes

CHAPTER SEVEN

Shadowboxing

Have you ever known someone just looking for a fight? No matter what you said or did, they were determined to see your actions as set against them or their stance on an issue. I have known folks like that, and to be honest, I have been that person myself as well. If there is one thing I have learned about life, it's that sometimes we can become the antagonist of our own storyline.

When I was young, I was not accustomed to seeing women in strong roles of authority. I was mostly surrounded by men. The language was driven toward men, and the opportunities absolutely came to the men only. As a young woman who knew she had a deep desire to lead not just women's ministry but also at a global level, I was definitely fighting an uphill battle.

My dad has three daughters, but he has not always seen us as capable leaders able to carry the weight of leadership to influence both men and women. That transformation took time in him. Because I was so accustomed to being around those who underestimated me as a woman, I found myself fighting for the seat at the table.

I fought over women having the privilege to perform weddings, funerals, ordinations, and become bishops. I would bow up at the slightest suspicion or intimation that someone was going to tell me I couldn't do something because I was a woman, or that it "wasn't my place."

Unfortunately, this did not produce a healthy view of men in my life, or a healthy response pattern. I started to view everything in my life through the lens of my adversity. I began to believe that I had to fight everyone who did not have the same perspective as I did on women in leadership (or any other point of disagreement), and that person would be an adversary to me and my mission.

This reached a new height with me one day when one of my colleagues was asked to speak to a group of leaders. He was invited to share about leading in an executive role when in reality, that function was where I led and led well.

He knew he was asked to participate in this particular setting because he was the male team member involved, not because he was more qualified or experienced. They were asking him to describe and expound on a job that I performed daily and he did not!

In that moment, I was so angry. I had worked hard to show myself approved, and I was still fighting off shadows of what I could or could not do. But God used that situation to reveal this truth to me. God said to me, "Amanda, I did not call you to be a fighter but a peacemaker. You are acting contrary to My nature and yours. Either you trust Me to do what I have put in your heart or you do not." It was in that critical moment with God that

He began to speak to me about the shadows I was aimlessly fighting.

This is my story, but for some of you, the story may be quite different. You may be a male leader who still cannot get in with the clique of hip pastors. Maybe you are a person who has been overlooked time and time again for a job promotion. I do know that shadow-making is not isolated to me alone.

Fighting Our Shadows

Many people are living out of a well of shadows that keep picking a fight with them. They approach everything from a protective stance because the shadows of their preconceived ideas and mistruths about themselves never leave. There is a voice constantly reiterating whatever "shadow" they have accepted and believe as truth. This causes them to feel like they must continually protect themselves and make sure no one, including God, is withholding from them.

I like to teach it this way: "I cannot empower anyone. Jesus already has given you power. I simply teach you how to unearth it." Empowerment has been liberally applied by academics and aid workers in the English-speaking world, including social services, social psychology, public health, adult literacy, and community development.[31] The idea of self-empowerment has become a major seller of books, podcasts, and conferences. The issue with that type of empowerment is that it implies someone or something is withholding from you. There is no need for empowerment unless the antithesis is present.

Here lies the problem. Once you believe God is withholding from you through His own actions or through others, you can easily become a fighter and not even know it.

Paul described the faith life as a race that he was not "running aimlessly" (1 Corinthians 9:26). I do not take lightly the journey of this life, because it has eternal value far beyond what I can see now. Paul was trying to help the Corinthians see, through their competitive mentality, that this was not a race to throw away aimlessly. This race of life is valuable and requires much diligence. He even said he refused to go about this journey "shadowboxing"—fighting every whim that came along (1 Corinthians 9:26 NLT).

When we start to believe that God is withholding from us, either by His own actions or by someone else's actions toward us, we are no longer running the right race. We instead become a company of social activist shadow-boxers. Every day on social media, we are presented with opportunities to jump on a social agenda and take up a cause. From saving the bees to climate change, and everything in between, there is no shortage of places to join and become an "activist." There is nothing wrong with standing for what you believe in, but truthfully, we are oftentimes fighting fake battles with no real stake or spoils.

Have you ever seen your shadow? It is always disproportionate to your real self. It can be wider, longer, fat head, no neck, long arms, short legs—all sorts of weird distortions—but it is never the exact representation of your true form.

In the same way, we can develop shadows within ourselves. These shadows are not physically seen, but they are evident by the way we speak and act. Have you ever met people who call themselves activists but the moment you disagree with them, they can no longer be your friend? Or maybe someone who posts depressing things on social media and puts in the comment line, "But don't worry, I will be fine." Every time I encounter these types of behaviors, I almost immediately know they are fighting a shadow.

People fighting shadows need approval. They are driven to find approval because whatever hidden shadow they are fighting is wearing them down.

Shadows in our lives are much like natural ones. These shadows are always bigger, longer, and look different than the actual form itself. Paul describes these shadows as "imaginations" (2 Corinthians 10:5 KJV).

Recently, Jason had to have some dental work done. When he got home from the dentist office, his face was not even swollen. He looked completely normal, but whenever I would talk to him, he constantly mentioned feeling weird. From his perspective, his face was huge and his entire jaw bigger on one side than the other, because of how it felt due to the numbing medication. From my perspective, I could not tell anything was out of the ordinary, based on his outward appearance.

When we are fighting shadow in our lives, we may seem like everything is okay on the surface but internally, we are dealing with bigger issues. These shadows feel overwhelming, and we feel like everyone else sees this glaring flaw within us. We are the only ones who can feel the numbing sensation—the shadows that are always hanging over our heads.

When we start fighting shadows and running our race with aimlessness, we will look for the wrong affirmations and earthly empowerments to secure us or commend us. We begin to act like we have numbing agents at work in our lives. We begin to operate out of the place that Paul called "shadowboxing."

Self-Control

Shadows are created by objects that impede light. The Bible describes God Himself as light. Psalm 36:9 says, "For with you is the fountain of life; in your light we see light" (NIV). John says of Jesus in John 1:9 that He was "the true light, which gives light to every man … coming into the world" (ESV). Jesus is the light. His Word lights the path for us (Psalm 119:105).

Shadows occur when we start letting other things get in front of Jesus in our lives. When we find ourselves in a position of shadowboxing, we must ask what is blocking the light of Christ in our life and circumstance. When we let our situations, our relationships, our motivations, our judgments, our circumstances, our family, our jobs, our business, or any area of our lives get in front of Jesus on our journey, we will always struggle to see clearly. We are hindering the lamp of God in our lives from fully shining on us and the path God has planned for us.

In Genesis 1:4, God separated light from dark, day from night. God eliminated shadows simply by separating them from each other. The Bible says of God that in Him is no "shadow of turning" (James 1:17 NKJV). God does not dwell in the shadows, but in the light.

Why is it, then, that we often find ourselves fighting shadows even though our desire is to live in the light of God? One reason is that we do not regard or guard our thought life as we should. How you think matters. What you do with your thoughts will determine how much light guides your life.

Second Corinthians 10:5 says it is our responsibility to bring "every thought into captivity to the obedience of Christ" (NKJV). You do not have to believe everything you think. Thoughts can come and go. We must oversee the thoughts we allow to come and stay, because those are the thoughts that shape our life. We must hold ourselves accountable for our thought life and submit our thoughts to the Lord.

Paul likened this type of accountability to that of an athlete who strives to obtain a prize through self-restraint and discipline. He used the term "temperate" to describe this characteristic (1 Corinthians 9:25 NKJV). To be temperate does not mean that you are a pushover, but rather that you can govern your own life without external controls. You possess the ability to monitor yourself, to sacrifice and deny your own desires for the end goal.

For an athlete to compete, they must have strong self-discipline. They do not get to sleep in every day, eat what they want, and show up to practice when it is convenient to their calendar. Athletes must prepare, condition, possess boundaries, and live with temperance.

One of the least-discussed fruits of the Spirit today is self-control. Everyone seems to want to skip right over that fruit! We want peace, joy, love, and goodness. Who doesn't?

When it comes to self-control and longsuffering, we tend to lose sight. Our culture has grown accustomed to hoping for the manifestation of the fruit without carrying the responsibility of developing it.

To develop any fruit of the Spirit, the Holy Spirit must have permission to work in the sensitive and difficult areas of our lives. It is not easy work. Self-control is usually one of these areas. To have self-control is to deny our desires from leading our decisions. It is the ability to hold our tongue, hold our peace, and hold our hope in tension.

Self-control is a spiritual fruit because it is a lifelong spiritual discipline. Joseph clearly had self-control in the book of Genesis. He was maligned on numerous occasions and then met his brothers in a season when he could have wiped them out and gotten revenge for the harm they had brought to his life. Joseph exercised self-control and ended up saving a nation and his own family.

Samson is a great cautionary tale about the importance of self-control. He was a fierce warrior and had an incredible line of victories. He was a great leader for the Israelites, with one major hang-up: he could not rule his own spirit when it really counted. From the beginning of his mother's pregnancy, she was instructed not to eat anything unclean, take wine, or cut his hair according to their customs. Samson ended up breaking all three of these restrictions with disastrous results.

In our world today, people feel more at liberty than ever to share "their truth" or "live freely." This liberty has popped up in every corner of our society. Yet there is a difference between freedom of speech as a citizen of a nation and freedom to live as Christ lives as a citizen of His kingdom.

Just because something is lawful for you does not mean it is helpful or healthy for you. Just because you *can* does not mean you *should*. Self-control is a discipline you develop through relationship with the Holy Spirit. The more the Holy Spirit works in your life, the more you develop life habits that may seem contrary to your natural rights but are born from within your heavenly citizenship.

When Paul talked about being temperate, he was describing this type of self-control. Paul did not have to say everything he was thinking. Nor did he trust everything he thought. This is evident in Romans 7:19, when Paul wrote, "For the good that I will to do, I do not do; but the evil I will not to do, that I practice" (NKJV).

Even Paul, one of the patriarchs of our faith, struggled to keep himself in alignment in both thought and deed. The difference was that he knew he could not think like God thinks just by going to church or reading a scroll or two. Paul knew it took the Holy Spirit at work in him. He had to discipline himself to apply what God thinks to his situation. He had to allow God's thoughts to override his natural reactions or thoughts.

Many people want to change the world, and so many more would if they would simply apply the discipline needed to do it. Most unfulfilled potential does not lie dormant due to the lack of opportunity but rather because of a lack of self-discipline to grasp the opportunity. Paul was so aware of his opportunity and the eternal value of that opportunity that he chose to discipline himself. He put down distractions, eliminated negative talk, and walked over impositions that would come to try to sway or rob from him. He developed self-control.

We need to acquaint ourselves with self-control once again, in our thought life and in our actions. Joyce Meyer explains the importance of self-control with our thought life. She calls it the "battlefield of the mind."[32] What occurs on that battlefield does not remain in our minds alone; it plays out in our daily actions. If I think I am incapable, I will not give my best effort. If I believe I have something to offer, I will not let people treat me like dirt. If I believe church is essential to my life, then I will not make excuses to miss services that will encourage my faith. You become what you believe. Your life reflects what you believe. Choose your thoughts wisely.

Seeing the Truth

Most people do not live out of reality. Most people live out of their perceived version of that reality. These perceptions become their moral guide and conscious meter. Their views of a situation are led by their subconscious desires for a specific outcome. We end up fighting shadows of things out of this place.

Like Jason at the dentist, we no longer see in the fullness of God; we only see in the narrowness of man. This is our challenge—to broaden how we view life to God's perspective, not our own. This is growth. When you grow, you can see things you did not see before.

It is like taking off in an airplane looking out the window at the terminal versus looking at the same field and buildings from 30,000 feet in the air. Your perspective diminishes those large objects on the ground, and your horizons broaden.

Isaiah 55:8 says, "'For My thoughts are not your thoughts, nor are your ways My ways,' says the LORD" (NKJV). God has better thoughts for us. If we want to stop fighting shadows and alternate realities, we must go higher and see as God sees. When we start to see as God sees, our view of everything going on around us changes.

One of the greatest tragedies is to watch people fight shadows in their lives year after year because they refuse to see their life from God's point of view. I watch them swing their boxing gloves at "what ifs" or "I think they are talking about me" types of things all the time. As a result, people end up living defeated because they are trapped by their own thoughts. Their actions then follow suit.

At one time, I let the shadow of my "right to be equal" stand in front of the light of God in my life. I lost perspective and sensitivity to the Holy Spirit. In that season, I no longer judged the circumstances around me with fresh eyes from a higher viewpoint but with the narrow eyes of critique. My actions became protection mechanisms, and my words at times critical, because I was fighting the shadows of a perceived reality.

God did not need any help moving me toward His purpose for my life. I was the one who had a hard time allowing Him. It has been my heart now for the past fifteen years to help others get the shadows out of the way so they can walk in the light and quit fighting shadows as well.

Make this a checkpoint for your life. Take hold of your thought life, no longer leaving your thoughts unchecked. Bring every "imagination" into submission (2 Corinthians 10:5 KJV) to the Holy Spirit so that you will no longer convince yourself of "truths" that may be factual but are not God-given truth. Guard your tongue and your heart more astutely. Put a bridle on your tongue and become temperate in all things. Stop before you speak. Steward your emotional life.

God redeemed our emotions at the cross. He took the old us and made us into something brand new. He put a new song in our hearts. He made us righteous for His name's sake. But, although He redeemed our emotions, we are still responsible to steward them well.

How do you steward your emotions so that you do not fight imaginary shadows? First, you renew your mind. Paul encouraged us in Romans 12:2, "Do not conform to the pattern of this world, but be transformed by the renewing of your mind" (NIV).

Daily life affects us. There are always opportunities for shadows to get in our way. We must renew our minds to keep proper perspective. One way to renew your mind is to stay in the Word of God (see Ephesians 5:26). Read your Bible. You cannot combat the shadows in your thought life from the Scripture you hear once a week during a church service.

Read your Bible every day. If you do not know where to start, begin in Proverbs and the Gospels and work from there. Reading the Bible helps you stay in alignment with God's thinking about you and our world. His Word is active and sharper than any two-edged sword. It is moving and activating and sharp enough to cut through any atmosphere around us. You must not forsake reading God's Word.

God also helps us renew our minds through right relationships and partnerships. I cannot tell you how valuable partnership has been to me in my journey. Just recently, I was facing some incredible challenges. I was hosting an event that seemed to have one reason after another pop up to cancel, but a partner spoke up and said, "You were made for this. If Jesus can go after the one, we can do this for the ones we have." Those words struck a chord with me. I pulled myself right up out of the depressive place I was wallowing in and got back to the planning. Sometimes a godly friend will help you renew your mind. Surround yourself with people who will point you back to the truth of the Word of God.

Stop Trying to Get Full Fighting Empty Things!

Muhammad Ali once said, "I have watched George Foreman shadowboxing and the shadow won."[33] Now, if you are a George Foreman fan, you will have to forgive me, but I could not think of a more appropriate line to attach to this next truth.

When you fight shadows, you never win, and you never lose. You end up fighting against something that never gets knocked out, yet completely wears you out in the process! The enemy of your life would like nothing better than to get you on his roller coaster ride and emotionally wear you down fighting empty battles.

The book of Daniel says of the enemy of the children of Israel that "he will speak words against the Most High [God] and wear down the saints of the Most High" (Daniel 7:25 AMP). It is always the plan of the enemy to wear people down. In words commonly attributed to General George S. Patton or coach Vince Lombardi, "Fatigue makes a coward out of all of us." Fatigue is certainly a tool in the enemy's hand, especially if it is attached to cycles of empty fighting.

When we feel defeated, we start to live in a constant state of what if, worry, and anxiety over who we are and where we belong. The enemy of our lives wants to keep us fighting this way because it is unproductive. It is the rocking chair syndrome: we are moving but making no progress. It is soothing, but it is not advancing anything in our lives. We have to overcome the schemes of the enemy by no longer engaging in unproductive fights. We have to stop shadowboxing!

You are reading this book post-2020. Oh, 2020—the year that so many people around the world shared similar, unfamiliar challenges because of the coronavirus pandemic. People have been faced with unpredictable changes, constantly adapting environments, and crazy learning curves.

When these kinds of adjustments are swirling around like a whirlwind, it is easy to become fatigued trying to keep all the tops spinning. But God never called us to keep all the tops spinning or to fight every shadow that pops up. God calls us to be victorious. In fact, it is an insult to God when we do not live in the victory He secured for us. We are a chosen generation, a royal priesthood, a holy nation!

When you feel low or worn down, take a minute to assess your heart and life. Ask yourself, "Am I fighting a shadow, or is this something I have been assigned to?" You can never get full by fighting empty things. You can never find your completion in winning some fight. You can never secure hope by getting all your ducks in a row. Trust me—someone or something will come along and disrupt those little ducks.

Fullness comes from knowing who you are in Christ and why you are on this planet, and by walking with the Holy Spirit in it! This is fullness. You do not need the right job—you need the right environment. You do not have to have a spouse to find what you need in life—you already have the One who sticks closer than a brother.

This is what you need to be full: Pick yourself up. Realize that you are the only one who can remove the shadows and let the light shine in. Let His light shine on every part of your world! Let the brilliance of Him overtake you and banish the shadows for good.

WORKBOOK

Chapter Seven Questions

Do I trust God in this? When you feel worn down, take a moment to assess your heart and life.

_____

_____

_____

_____

_____

_____

_____

_____

_____

_____

_____

Who does God say I am? What are you trying to prove? Who are you trying to impress? Whose opinion has taken precedence over what God says about you?

_____
_____
_____
_____
_____
_____
_____
_____
_____
_____

Who do I say I am? Write down three attributes that make you unique and wonderful. Thank God for making you who you are!

_____
_____
_____
_____
_____
_____

Chapter Seven Notes

CHAPTER EIGHT

Growing Over It in Hope

There is an interesting segment of time in biblical history that not many people may be familiar with, often referred to by scholars as the four hundred years of silence. This period of silence occurred between the last book of the Old Testament, Malachi, and the first book of the New Testament, Matthew. Many people refer to it as the four hundred years of silence because there were no new books of the Bible, no scholarly insight, and no prophetic words from God recorded during this span of time.[34]

At the close of the book of Malachi, the writer shared a prophetic word about the coming Messiah. The Israelites were now back in Palestine under Persian control.[35] They were once again truly a minority in the land. When the book of Matthew began, the balance of power in the ancient world had shifted west. Things had changed. Greek was now the primary language of the day, and the Septuagint had been written, which was the Greek translation of the Old Testament. Rome had become the center of authority, and Herod the Great was the ruling king in Palestine.

This was a dark and turbulent time in history for the Israelites, by now called Jews. They lived under the thumb of some major disruptions. They were a small nation caught in the cross hairs of some big players. It would have been difficult for the Israelites to believe that God was present with them during such unrest, turmoil, and persecution. Times were dark for their people, and God seemed distant and silent.

The first chapter of Matthew opens with an interesting genealogy of Joseph. A genealogy is a line of descendants traced from their ancestors—basically, the tracing of one's history through the family name, or tracking the family tree. Matthew made a point of connecting Joseph and his family to the coming Messiah. He went even further in his account to connect the reality that even though many national and historical events took place in those silent years between Malachi and his book, God was anything but silent.

During captivity, nations were overthrown, people imprisoned and enslaved, and wars waged over territory, but Matthew kept the genealogy of Jesus in the forefront. The lineage of God's redemptive purpose never stopped. God was still working in the dark seasons to bring forth what Galatians calls the "fullness of the time" through His chosen people (Galatians 4:4 NKJV).

God felt no obligation to explain those four hundred years of silence. He never addressed them. All God did through the hand of Matthew was record the next son in the genealogy. You may ask what that has to do with anything? To me, this is one of the greatest expressions of God's steadfast nature. Yes, Israel had been captured. Yes, they lived without a king, and then with an ungodly one. Yes, the Israelites got themselves into quite a mess with new laws and poor priest selections, but despite all of that, God kept moving His Word forward through the genealogy.

This exemplifies exactly why we must never get caught up in thinking that just because God is not doing something in a way we think He should that He is not with us. He is always moving His Word forward. When He declares a thing, time immediately starts marching toward its fulfillment.

Real Hope

Maybe you can identify with this story. You have felt like you have been caught between two seasons and faced the pain of turbulent times. I want to encourage you that God is not a God who disappoints. He is committed to His Word. Psalm 138:2 says, "Yes, you made your word even greater than your name" (EHV). God honors His Word. God knows that His name is great and His Word is even greater. Even though the world at the end of the Old Testament seemed dark and lost, and the years following were quiet, God was still birthing hope on the earth. His Word was still working.

Hope is the underlying force in this scenario and in our lives. Hope is never based on what you can see, but rather on what you cannot see. It is of no value to hope for something that is evident in full form. That is not real hope. According to Hebrews 11:1, our faith is birthed in our ability to hope for the unseen things. It is advanced vision. Hope is seeing in the dark. Secondly, hope is not conditional. Romans 5:5 says, "Now hope does not disappoint, because the love of God has been poured out in our hearts by the Holy Spirit who has been given to us" (NKJV). Hope is linked to the love of God, which is steadfast and eternal. Hope anchors us to the immutability of God (Hebrews 6:18–19 NKJV) and holds us up in spite of the darkness.

In Matthew 1, we see that God was not nearly as silent as everyone thought He was. He was not speaking to His prophets as He had done previously, but He was still very present and active. His Word was being manifested in consistent action we could all take for granted. He was working His promises through the family unit in Israel, birthing one generation to the next rather than speaking another prophetic word.

To have real hope is to believe in God's ways. We must release our preferences on how they come to pass. If we cannot embrace the mysterious ways of God, we may miss out on what He is doing on the earth.

Third, hope brings endurance. First Thessalonians 1:3 says, "We remember before our God and Father your work produced by faith, your labor prompted by love, and your endurance inspired by hope in our Lord Jesus Christ" (NIV). When you have hope, you capture endurance. If you do not know why you are doing something, you will not continue to do it.

Hope gives us the why. It centers our attention on God's big picture, not our mini portraits. Hebrews 10:36 says we have "need of endurance" (ESV). When we allow hope to arise in our hearts, we begin to feel courage arise as well, and this brings to us the ability to keep going.

To grow over it, we must be people of hope. Paul wrote in Ephesians that his prayer for them was that the "eyes of [their[heart[s] become enlightened so [they] may know what is the hope of His calling" (CSB). When we are growing over it, this needs to be our prayer as well. We must ask that the eyes of our heart be enlightened so we can know the hope we have in Jesus.

When we become aware of who God really is in the story, we will stop questioning the ending. God is not writing your story beginning to end but end to beginning. He remains in control if you let Him. His outcomes are always sweeter than we ever could have imagined. When we pray that the eyes of our heart are enlightened, we are praying that God will remind us who He is in the storyline. He is not a character—He is the author! He knows the end from the beginning.

How to Have Hope in the Silence

There are three ways we can learn to be enlightened in the hope of Jesus in the middle of seasons that seem silent around us:

1. We must become confident in the unseen things. I am a little bit of a documentary geek, and I love to watch documentaries on the exploration of space. Recently, I was watching a *National Geographic* documentary on the telescope and its evolution in space science. Interestingly, in the midst of the interviews, one of the scientists mentioned that they no longer use telescopes to locate things in space. Instead, they now watch for the effects on what they can see so that they can become more aware of what they cannot see.

Scientists have discovered that space is far bigger than they imagined. There is more space that they cannot see than they can see. The only way to become aware of what they cannot see is by observing its effects on what they can see. Second Corinthians 4:18 tells us, "So we fix our eyes not on what is seen, but on what is unseen" (NIV).

Have you ever heard of dark matter? In the 1970s, the American astronomer Vera Rubin, picking up an idea pitched by Swiss astronomer Franz Zwicky a few decades before, suggested that there must be extra matter in and around the galaxies—perhaps ten times more than what we can see—holding everything together. This has come to be called dark matter. The thought behind dark matter is that when astronomers study what we can see and understand, we become increasingly aware that something else has to be at work in it, because on its own there is no way it could happen.[36]

Whether you believe in the theory of dark matter or not, there is definitely something in the unseen holding our spinning galaxy of stars in place. In the same way the telescope awakened us to our galactic findings, hope awakens us in our life. People should be able to look at you and wonder, "There is no way she is holding it together?" or, "How in the world is he able to stay the course in the midst of this storm?"

Just like the dark matter theory, there is an unseen force holding your galaxy in place, too. It becomes apparent in what others can see about you, that something is at work on your behalf helping to hold things together. Hebrews 1:3 says, "The Son is the radiance of God's glory and the exact expression of his nature, sustaining all things by his powerful word" (CSB). This verse says that God's Word is over you and your world and He is holding you up by its power. Let your heart be enlightened to this great hope!

The unseen is never an indication of God's absence but most often an indication of God's displayed work in us. When others see us growing over it in hope, they see the unseen at work, too! It is the hope of His Word working on our behalf.

2. We establish that God is the sole source and provider of hope in our lives. When we are feeling lost or misunderstood, we often look to artificial forms of hope in our lives. We look to our spouse or to achievements. We look to friends or hobbies or our children. We look for a season shift or a new venture. However, the result is always the same.

Hope is never sustained in any of these things because real hope can only be originated in God. Paul wrote to the Romans, "May the God of hope fill you with all joy and peace as you trust in him, so that you may overflow with hope by the power of the Holy Spirit" (Romans 15:13 NIV). God is hope. God does not just carry the characteristic of hope; He is hope.

When the God of hope shows up, He never comes alone. Romans tells us that we serve a God who originated hope by being hope and, further, He brings additional blessings with this hope. He fills us with joy and peace. I like what Charles Spurgeon says: "Peace is joy resting, and joy is peace dancing."[37] He describes joy is an "inward satisfaction"[38] and peace as "settled."[39] I see joy as that "inward satisfaction." Nothing satisfies you like knowing you are a King's kid! Peace is feeling settledness in knowing that not only are you a King's kid, but you are also a wanted, valued part of the family.

When God's hope comes to our lives, He brings with it an ability to be content in our circumstances and an ability to be settled about who is in control of them. Even when the children of Israel were in Babylonian captivity, God still was bringing hope to them:

> *"For I know the plans I have for you," declares the LORD, "plans to prosper you and not to harm you, plans to give you hope and a future.*
> —*Jeremiah 29:11* NIV

3. We must let hope anchor us. Hope helps to calm our troubled soul. It anchors the drifting that could easily enter our life. Hebrews 6:19 says, "This hope we have as an anchor of the soul, both sure and steadfast, and which enters the Presence behind the veil" (NKJV).

God knows that drifting can happen in our lives. When I read Hebrews 6:19, I get the reassuring sense that when we feel the drifting, we open our eyes to the hope that anchors our souls. Drifting is not necessarily backsliding or relinquishing our faith, but rather a slow process of loss of expectation.

I can still remember taking a raft out on the Gulf Coast and laying out on it, not too far from the shore, enjoying the water and sunshine. My mom started yelling at me to watch what I was doing because I was not anchored to the seafloor. I was simply drifting on the ocean, and if I did not pay attention, I could end up farther out than I meant to go. Likewise, the current of life will take your raft in many different directions if you are living unanchored.

In the New Testament, there is a story of comparison about a life built on the sand and one built upon the rock. Both are described to have encountered wind and waves. Both endured a storm, but according to the story, only one survived it (Matthew 7:24–29). I am sure if you are not familiar with the story, you still guessed which one: the one that survived was built on the rock.

Interestingly, sand and rock are similar substances. The difference is, one substance is whole and one is divided and split into pieces. It is the compact, intact substance—the rock—that survived the storm, not the disjointed one.

We too often try to anchor ourselves to un-whole things in our lives. Wrong relationships, wrong expectations of our jobs, and wrong perspectives on God can all be disjointed and unstable, causing us to have faulty foundations. When people do not see God working in them, they try by default to fill the void of what they do not see with what they can see. They tend to rely on the things they can control.

The story of the two houses shows us that both were builders. One built on the right things while the other built on the wrong things. It is of no consequence to have built a house if it will not stand the test of the winds and waves. It still takes time to build a house, even on a faulty foundation. Drifting also does not happen instantaneously. It happens over time as we slowly give up our expectation in God for known things we can control.

God wants us to learn to anchor our lives to Him in hope and to stop placing our hope in the wrong foundations. "This hope we have as an anchor." Our hope is what we use to stop our drifting and stop our building on faulty foundations. When we are feeling like the storm is moving us in directions we should not be headed, we do not need to complain. Often this is just the opportunity for God to awaken hope in us again, in a new place!

Many of us have walked in a season between the two books—the four hundred years of silence—or are experiencing that even now. You can be full of hope for the future and still questioning the waiting. Silent times are not necessarily inactive times. Often these times are the most productive seasons toward our purpose.

The question becomes, are the eyes of your heart enlightened enough to see that God is at work, even if it is just the genealogy of your life? The generations that held hope and kept faith during the silent years did their part to make a way for the "fullness of the time" to come. God wastes nothing. His fullness of time over your life will come. Stay anchored to hope, because you are growing over the wall!

WORKBOOK

Chapter Eight Questions

Do I trust God in this? What does it look like for you to operate in hope?

_____
_____
_____
_____
_____
_____
_____
_____
_____
_____
_____

Who does God say I am? What do you know to be true about God and your identity in Him? How does that increase your faith and hope?

_____

_____

_____

_____

_____

_____

_____

_____

_____

Who do I say I am? How can you speak the truth over your circumstances with hope and confident faith?

_____

_____

_____

_____

_____

_____

Chapter Eight Notes

CONCLUSION

Choose Trust

If you abide in Me, and My words abide in you, you will ask what you desire, and it shall be done for you. By this My Father is glorified, that you bear much fruit; so you will be My disciples.
—**John 15:7–8** NKJV

When the famine was raging, Joseph's brothers came to Egypt to ask for food. They didn't recognize the man in charge of passing out food as their little brother. Why would they? They'd sold him off as a slave. It was almost impossible that he'd become such a powerful man.

And here Joseph faced the hardest obstacle yet: he had to choose to forgive his brothers. These men were now begging Joseph for help. Their lives were now in *his* hands. Had Joseph pictured a moment like this when he was carried away, sold to slavers? Had he fantasized about avenging himself on these men when he was languishing in prison?

But Joseph had a distinct advantage. All those years

ago, at the start of things, he'd had a dream from God that this very thing would happen. He'd dreamed that his brothers would bow down before him. And sure enough, here they were, bowing in deference to the second most powerful man in Egypt. Joseph knew God brought it about. He knew all of the things that happened in his life had been for God's glory.

God is calling you to do the same thing. Your life won't be as dramatic as Joseph's, I hope, but you will certainly face obstacles. It will be tempting to focus all your attention on the obstacle and stop seeing that God is standing right beside you, calling you to Him.

Dream God's dreams. Abide in Him faithfully. Let Him prune away the withered branches. Overcome rejection. Take your boxing gloves off and fix your eyes on God. Let the life of Joseph teach you how to grow over the obstacles. Choose to trust the good Gardener when hardship comes your way.

And how will you know when you've succeeded? Well, you'll have good fruit growing on your vines. You'll face adversity and put your hand right into God's, trusting that He'll work things out to His glory. Fear will have no place in your life. You will live in victory and no longer be a victim. Your vine will grow over the wall and produce beautiful fruit that remains for the glory of God. So go ahead and grow over it!

REFERENCES

Notes

1. *Blue Letter Bible,* "Strong's G4395 – prophēteuō." https://www.blueletterbible.org/lexicon/g4395/kjv/tr/0-1/.

2. *Blue Letter Bible,* "Strong's G2307 – thēlema." https://www.blueletterbible.org/lexicon/g2307/kjv/tr/0-1/.

3. American-Israeli Cooperative Enterprise. "Charity (Tzedekah): Charity Throughout Jewish History." Jewish Virtual Library. https://www.jewishvirtuallibrary.org/charity-throughout-jewish-history.

4. Johnson, Bill. At the Issachar Initiative Conference, Church on the Living Edge, Orlando, FL, 2018.

5. *Britannica,* "St. Paul's Contributions to the New Testament." By Melissa Petruzzello. https://www.britannica.com/list/st-pauls-contributions-to-the-new-testament.

6. TOW Project. "1 Corinthians and Work." Theology of Work. https://www.theologyofwork.org/new-testament/1-corinthians

7. Knittel, Marvin. "The Story of the Dipper and the Bucket."

Psychology Today. https://www.psychologytoday.com/us/blog/how-help-friend/201703/the-story-the-dipper-and-the-bucket.

8. Maraboli, Steve. *Unapologetically You: Reflections on Life and the Human Experience*. Better Today Publishing, 2013.

9. Harvard Health Publishing. "Anxiety and Stress Weighing Heavily at Night? A New Blanket Might Help." March 2019. https://www.health.harvard.edu/mind-and-mood/anxiety-and-stress-weighing-heavily-at-night-a-new-blanket-might-help.

10. *Lexico,* "stagnation." https://www.lexico.com/definition/stagnation.

11. *Encyclopedia of the Bible,* "Shiloh." Bible Gateway. https://www.biblegateway.com/resources/encyclopedia-of-the-bible/Shiloh.

12. Ellicott, Charles, ed. *A Bible Commentary for English Readers*. Cassell & Company, 1905.

13. *Bible Hub,* "ephod." https://biblehub.com/topical/e/ephod.htm.

14. *Merriam-Webster,* "thief." https://www.merriam-webster.com/dictionary/thief.

15. *Merriam-Webster,* "rob." https://www.merriam-webster.com/dictionary/robber.

16. *Latin Is Simple,* "reicere." https://www.latin-is-simple.com/en/vocabulary/verb/6013/.

17. Brown, Brené. *Dare to Lead: Brave Work, Tough Conversations, Whole Hearts*. Random House, 2018, p. 9.

18. Lokos, Allan. *Pocket Peace: Effective Practices for Enlightened Living*. Penguin Publishing Group, 2010.

19. Sweet, Leonard. *What Matters Most: How We Got the Point but Missed the Person.* Crown Publishing Group, 2012.

20. Elliot, Elisabeth. *Shadow of the Almighty.* HarperCollins, 1989, p. 91.

21. *Gesenius' Hebrew–Chaldee Lexicon.* In *Blue Letter Bible,* "Strong's H7965 – šālôm." https://www.blueletterbible.org/lexicon/h7965/kjv/wlc/0-1/.

22. Graham, Franklin, and Donna Lee Toney. *Billy Graham in Quotes.* Thomas Nelson, 2011.

23. Graham and Toney, *Billy Graham in Quotes.*

24. *Dictionary.com,* "hostile." https://www.dictionary.com/browse/hostile.

25. *Lexico,* "wind." https://www.lexico.com/en/definition/wind.

26. *Bible Hub,* "2570. kalos." https://biblehub.com/greek/2570.htm.

27. Elliot, Elisabeth. *Through Gates of Splendor.* Harper & Brothers, 1957.

28. Elliot, *Shadow of the Almighty.*

29. *Blue Letter Bible,* "Strong's H7971 – šālaḥ." https://www.blueletterbible.org/lang/lexicon/lexicon.cfm?Strongs=H7971&t=KJV.

30. *Blue Letter Bible,* "Isaiah 6." https://www.blueletterbible.org/kjv/isa/6/8/t_conc_685008.

31. Simon, Barbara Levy. *The Empowerment Tradition in American Social Work.* Columbia University Press, 1994.

32. Meyer, Joyce. *Battlefield of the Mind Bible: Renew Your Mind*

Through the Power of God's Word. FaithWords, 2017.

33. BBC. "Muhammad Ali – in His Own Words." June 4, 2016. https://www.bbc.com/sport/boxing/16146367?ocid=socialflow_facebook&ns_mchannel=social&ns_campaign=bbcnews&ns_source=facebook.

34. Got Questions Ministries. "What Were Israel's 400 Years of Silence?" Compelling Truth. https://www.compellingtruth.org/400-years-of-silence.html.

35. Swindoll, Chuck. "Malachi." Insight for Living Ministries. https://www.insight.org/resources/bible/the-minor-prophets/malachi.

36. Childers, Tim. "The Astronomer Who Brought Dark Matter to Light." Space.com. June 11, 2019. https://www.space.com/vera-rubin.html.

37. Spurgeon, Charles Haddon. "A Round of Delights." In *Metropolitan Tabernacle Pulpit,* vol. 23. The Spurgeon Center. https://www.spurgeon.org/resource-library/sermons/a-round-of-delights/#flipbook/.

38. Spurgeon, Charles Haddon. "A Happy Christian." In *Metropolitan Tabernacle Pulpit,* vol. 13. The Spurgeon Center. https://www.spurgeon.org/resource-library/sermons/a-happy-christian/#flipbook/.

39. Spurgeon, Charles Haddon. "Peace: A Fact and a Feeling." In *Metropolitan Tabernacle Pulpit,* vol. 25. The Spurgeon Center. https://www.spurgeon.org/resource-library/sermons/peace-a-fact-and-a-feeling/#flipbook/.

About the Author

Amanda comes from a long line of great leaders and, with over two decades of experience herself, is not a newbie at the table of leadership. Amanda truly embodies what it means to be a leader to leaders; she is an encourager to the underdog, a coach to the growing, and a faith-filled developer of the future. As a pastor of a growing congregation in England and an international speaker, Amanda continues to pour her life into being a voice that can and will make a difference for Jesus. Amanda has a beautiful family she gets to do life with, and when she is not fulfilling assignments on the road or at home, she is taking on new adventures with her husband and three incredible children.

Printed in Dunstable, United Kingdom